DECLUTTER YOUR HOME

Letting go of all the stuff you don't need

NICK STURGEON

Bridgewater Ink

Published by Bridgewater Ink Limited

Contents

ONE

Starting Off

THANKS FOR PICKING up this book and exploring the ideas around the process of letting go of the stuff of your life that is holding you in a place where - I have to assume this - you don't actually want to be right now. For me, an inveterate hoarder, I challenged myself just this year to deal with the amassed possessions that have been filling shelves, cupboards, space below the stairs, and in the garage, with boxes, plastic containers and large holdalls and travel bags of unidentified possessions. It started when I was a boy and it has always been this way for me as a hoarder.

My partner and I were looking at the house we lived in and the space we had in our house versus the volume that we actually used and enjoyed. In addition to this we considered the areas of the house that we did not naturally invite visitors to see when they came round to spend time with us. We wanted to avoid them seeing the cluttered places and rooms.

The frightening realisation that we used only half of

the house space for our day to day activity lead us to make a bet with each other about what we could do to explore the mass of accumulated possessions. Could we instead look to live in either a clearer space where the energy would be brighter and more alive? How about moving to a smaller property, living without the clutter that had been dragged around with us over the years?

What sparked this decision to create the challenge at home? My favourite bookshop occupies one long floor of a beautifully and historic converted weaving mill, set alongside a railway line and right next to a canal, a river and a country park. I was browsing the shelves one weekend and my attention was caught by a beautiful clean copy of a title about decluttering. I sat on a reading bench with the book and began to go through it. The chapter titles drew me in to how I might better deal with my clothes by folding them in a special way, methods to calculate what represented the right number of shoes to keep, and questions around the levels of joy that an item brought to me. The book cover was white and very subtly projected the attractive image of a potentially clean and clutter free living environment. This promise was so good and I of course began to take it to the cash desk. Half way across the stripped wood floor of the gorgeous bookshop I found myself having an epiphany. *"What the hell was I doing buying a book about dealing with clutter, if only to take the book home and add yet more weight to an existing bookshelf?"*

My major clutter devil is my addiction to books. For years I have bought books almost as soon as I have touched them. In our home at the time I was about to buy that book at the till I already had around 2,500 books. If there were such a civil category then I would be classified as an official hoarder with serious kleptomaniac tendencies! There is in fact a psychological state of Hoarding Disorder, more of which I shall explain later.

Once I was asked by a friend to remove my stacks of books from their home loft out of fear that the ceiling below would collapse with the sheer weight of the boxed collections. She had kindly stored them for me when I lost my previous home and was struggling to find permanent accommodation. This kind lady had been sympathetic to the plight of my books and graciously allowed me to store them. In truth by the time I found a permanent place to call home I had pretty much forgotten what was in each of the boxes. It took fully eight car loads for me to remove the ninety six boxes and take them to my new place.

Guess where all of these boxes were when I decided on the declutter challenge that lead to the writing of this book? Yes, you are right. They were all in the garage and one of the outbuildings of our new home. They had gathered dust for years since the move and never been opened. Most of the boxes had been packed and sealed up a full five years previously.

To let go of anything requires a decision. To let go of our generic 'stuff' can be a difficult process for many of us given that the size of the task can be daunting. Somewhere in our head we know that we have too much. Too many food processing gizmos, too many magazines on home style, too many items of underwear, or winter coats, or gardening tools, or drinking glasses, or walking sticks, or reading glasses, or knives and forks. You get the idea because you know your own living space so very well. We watch TV shows about people living in tiny homes, or practicing a minimalist lifestyle which seems to require a yurt or a container home and we are put off. To be honest, the more I see the really good container homes online the more inspired I am by what can be done to shed the non-essentials and live better with less. So we know we can do better than this, but why do we continue to hold onto so much?

We understand that there is a link between the mass of 'stuff' and the emotional sense of feeling weighed down by it all. Yet still we buy and accumulate. If it was a logical process to make space for a new thing by clearing out the old before we go shopping, then our lives would be easy, our home spaces clutter free. It is not this way and so we must adapt and change our behaviour to meet the problem we have created for ourselves.

We attach feeling and meaning, nostalgia and memory to each item that stays on our shelves, in our cupboards and which hangs on our walls or has a special place on our window ledge. Many of the feelings and thoughts which we pin to the objects are deep rooted and we are unaware of the pull we have to the item. With another possession we might have a clear memory of the occasion when it was given to us and by whom. That memory can be good, bad, or downright unpleasant. Why are you hanging on to something which has anything other than a good sensation or memory attached to it?

You need to look at the benefits of decluttering and letting go, versus the negatives of hanging on to so much that you know is already draining you, making you feel heavy or even guilty around some things and simply unhappy about others. Keeping things that bring you no practical or emotional benefit can be a waste of your time, energy and a drain on your well-being. Whether we are considering a broken electrical item in your basement, or chipped and cracked crockery in your kitchen, the items are no good for you. It is not only the physical things in your living space.

Are you hanging on to old diaries containing entries that remind you of regret, sadness or failure? How about documents from a difficult job you walked away from or a business you closed down. These things each carry a stagnant energy which is not part of who you are now. The act of holding onto such things can pull you down and hold you back. Rather than hold onto so much that gives you no actual benefit, it's time to let it go out of your life. Through the act of letting go you are creating a positive space into which something new or beneficial can come.

What is the cost of your clutter?

In my example of the ninety six boxes, I had allowed a third of our house to be utilised by packed and boxed clutter. On a building that cost me £1,200 per month the maths are easy to do. This figure is the cost of living in the building, and also includes insurance, utilities as well as decoration. That's £400 per month of my outgoings spent each month on the storage value of my boxes, most of these containing books. That's £4,800 a year over five years minimum or £24,000 that I have shelled out as a part of my overall accommodation costs just to store several thousand books that I have not looked at or made any use of in that time. Boy, did this realisation make me feel stupid! It also caused me to feel real sadness that I had not handled the situation well.

In your own place what have you got that takes up the equivalent of at least a full room in your house? Think about the value of the items that you have in that combined space where, if you were to box all the 'stuff' and stack those boxes, you would end up with a room filled from floor to ceiling. Take that room as a proportion of your property and identify the monthly cost of that building or space. It doesn't really matter whether you rent or own and pay a mortgage. The cost you have is the cost. If the clutter is taking up 10% of your monthly accommodation budget then take that figure as you Cost of Clutter. If it is 20% then it is 20% of your expenditure. This fact should be enough to make you sit up and take notice all of a sudden.

I know you might say, *"But Nick, don't be hard on me! This is only filling the basement or a garage unit attached to the house."* Am I sympathetic to you? NO! Not at all. Am I empathetic to your situation? Yes, for sure I am. Having been through the process myself I am going to be hard on you throughout the book, so get used to this. I care enough to help you make the difference in your life that we finally had the courage to tackle in our own situation.

Whatever the cost, take a moment to see that same

amount of money in your savings account and being available to you for fun activities, investment, travel and holidays. The same money could be used to pay down or settle in full loans that you have and which you would like to be free and clear of. Consider the emotional relief that will come from taking such money and clearing those debts. You could equally use it to buy possessions that you genuinely love and adore, and which might have an investment value as well as being functional and or beautiful in your living space. Items that you would benefit from seeing and using every day. I guess I have your attention now, even if the suggestion that you calculate the actual cost of your clutter has hurt you.

This will not be easy, but the journey you can make is a simple one. We need to explore the items in your house that bring you no benefit or which have fulfilled the function for which you originally bought them. This usage or non usage relates only to some of the clutter in your life.

A lot more of it will be having an emotional cost to you. In the same way that I had in the back of my mind the subconscious sense of the emotional weight of those boxes of books, files and papers, so too will you also be carrying a burden associated with the stuff you are carrying about in your home space. I thought about the fact that they were filling a friends loft space. I worried about the time involved in moving them to a new place once I had found one. I had to take on board the cost of the house I would need in order to store all the items, and then of how to live my life in a house that was heavy (emotionally and physically) with the clutter that I brought with me to this new relationship and our jointly shared house.

And so it was I came home from the bookshop without a book, a very rare thing for me since books have always been my compulsion. I came through the front door and said *"We have to do something. I realise the level of my hoarding and am really embarrassed about it."* I was genuinely distressed at how out of control my book addiction had become and had fixated on this thought since driving back from the book store. My partner is kind and caring and understood. She simply said *"I've been waiting for you to realise this my love"*, and gave me the biggest and most forgiving hug. In that simple moment was born the start of our plan to declutter and live a lighter life, one without the burden of the clutter and the chaos it brings.

If you have become a clutter junky over time, then this journey is going to require you to be brave as we move along a path towards a home with less burden and more joy, to a place where you know what you have and where it is. If you simply have more stuff than you need to live a happy and fulfilling life, and cupboards and wardrobes bulging with stuff you neither use nor wear, then you will enjoy the practical satisfaction and emotional relief that comes with the letting go of the unwanted, the unneeded and the undesirable 'stuff' that is clogging the arteries of your living space.

Imagine the pleasure of coming home to a place where everything has its place and you know precisely where that place is. How much time do you lose in the course of just a week looking for things that are no longer where you imagined them to be and in struggling to consider how you might find them? Imagine also what might happen if, within your accumulated record of your life history, you find and reconnect with items that are in good order and have a value to someone else, that can be sold via online sites and where you can receive the financial value of such things with relative ease.

How do you calculate what might be there? You are going to have to find it, unpack it and make a list. What do you have? I have no idea. What did I find in my own storage boxes? In roughly 80 of the 96 boxes I had stored second hand books, books I had bought for their non-fiction value. With perhaps 20 books to a box that was 1,600 books I had been carrying around and hanging on to. Some of these boxes, only a few, had been damaged by water, or cold and were easy to throw away. But 1,600 books at a minimum purchase value of £5 represents £8,000 of money sitting around. In most cases I had looked through each book just once. So there was another £8,000 of money spent instead of invested. I argued with myself that I had received the value of the purchases, but of course was left with the certain knowledge that I had done nothing at all with the books since reading them.

Why do we gather clutter?

The reasons are many and often complicated and the exploration of these is going to open up that proverbial 'can of worms' as we work through these together. The power of emotions has the greatest hold on us as we delve into this topic and some of the reasons will astound you. At the very least you will be surprised by some of the learning you make in the process. Ask yourself :

"Why do I have Grandpa Tom's hand built coffee table in my life?"

"Does the clock on the wall that was on a mantelpiece in my long-dead Aunty's house need to have a place in my own living room, some twenty years after she passed?"

"Does the team football photograph that showed my Dad as a young man about to leave school seventy years ago need to be on the wall in my hallway?"

"Just because I was given a hand painted teapot and matching cups and saucers by my best man and his wife when we first married twenty five years ago - and divorced after twelve years - should I still have this on the shelf in my kitchen? Especially when I have not used it in the two years since we took it out of the box it was found in?"

These are random questions that I use from my own example of clutter and accumulated items in the challenge that we set ourselves at home. I am sure you can easily find your own relevant examples of things around you.

Here are a couple of simple questions for you today, intended purely to help you find your place in all of this.

Do you consider that you have all your possessions under control?

When you see the clutter in your house, whether on display in the common areas and daily used rooms of your home, or stuffed awkwardly into the lesser observed areas of cupboards, attics, basements or boxes in the garage, how does that make you feel?

Enough said! Your clutter is personal to you and your lifestyle as well as to your attitude and approach to life. Millions of other people live with everything they own under one roof and they experience no guilt or upset. But this exploration of letting go is not about them. I have confessed my own situation and how I felt that so many material things were draining my energy and time.

The things we bring into our home space should be there because they make tasks easier or to bring us happiness.

Where our possessions become so many that they are more than we can manage and they start to distract us from living the life we should be enjoying, this is where the trouble begins and the stress starts to wear us down. We work longer hours and spend more of our disposable income just to keep the possessions under control by such things as storage, insurance and taking on bigger and more costly spaces to live in.

Quite naturally, we need to place much of our focus on our home, on our living space and the things within it. But a full approach to letting go requires that we don't just limit ourselves only to mess and chaos, to clutter and junk as they appear in your physical world. We will also explore the damage that comes from being connected with toxic people, the distraction of digital clutter and the overwhelm that can come from addiction to gathering more around you than you need.

To answer the question of "Why do we gather clutter?" we do this because we are human. We do it because we feel we need to collect things around us so that we can make statements such as these :

"I am safe now".

"They are not making this quality any more, so let's get one now".

"I can provide for my family".

"I deserve to have this because I have gone through so much".

"Do you know how much I had to work this month?"

"This was a bargain, so I had to get it".

"We've been struggling recently so I figured we deserved this".

Being human gives us a sense that we have to carve out our own identity in a world that is so often homogenised, identical, similar brand - different perspective, must-have, latest trend, special item, but really very much the same. We think that by surrounding ourselves with the things which reflect who we believe ourselves to be in the world, we will then create a space which feels unique to us. And when you first do this, starting to accumulate the things around you which make you feel good, it does seem like you are achieving the goal of originality. But at what cost, or better said, at what price?

What price have you paid to fill your home with the things that you have purchased in order to bring home and just to say *"This coat is me"* or *"These books and this desk are me"* or *"This car is me".* Some of that is your own voice and heart talking. However, there will be a proportion of 'stuff' in your dwelling space which has got in there, easily or by pushing it's way in, because of advertising, because of the cultural influence of your neighbourhood or peer group, of social media and what is or is not 'on-trend' this week. Letting go of this stuff will emotionally and physically open up space in your home. While it can seem like a push to make the decision to look at each thing we have and bag or box it for discarding or donating, the value of you doing so is beyond measure.

As we go on this declutter journey together, there will be opportunities to work through various exercises and activities. All voluntary of course. One very probable realisation is likely to be that your early dreams and aspirations for what home should look like, but also feel like, will make themselves very clear to you. Some of these will have been completely forgotten over previous years, others will whisper gently and kindly to you and ask to be let back into your living space to reflect all those good aspects of you, your character and your values. Welcome them when you see them, as you surely will when you reduce the distraction that has been overwhelming your personal space.

TWO

Living the lighter life

AT WHAT POINT this past month did you think about your home and living space and wish you had less? I am willing to lay money down that this was not an idea to consider a month ago, and might even have been as recent a thought as today. Not because you are looking at a book on this theme of Letting Go, but because the idea has been a prominent one in your mind for a long time.

Consider these very simple situations :

If the world gave you a year's income today could you get on a flight next week and not look back to your home and possessions while you are away?

If a dear friend called you tonight and invited you to join them on the other side of the world for a three month adventure, with all your expenses paid for travel and accommodation, could you join them this weekend?

If you get into work next Monday and your employer gives you the news that your entire department is closing down, (and assuming your own finances are good and you have savings for the project) can you lock the door on your home and possessions, leaving them behind for a full month of training or education you have wanted to attend since you learned about it a year ago?

In each scenario we are assuming that the bills are taken care of, that finances are no reason for you to avoid the opportunity to enjoy yourself. If the money is not an issue and you have the confidence to take part in the adventure and you have the freedom in your calendar, why are you not doing these things?

Most households - and you might be one of them - are trapped by the burden of not being in control of their possessions. You cannot lock the door on your practical ownership of clutter and junk to take off and enjoy yourself. You couldn't rent out your home for a longer trip, because the chaos is everywhere and way too much for a guest to live with. You can't invite guests to stay for even a weekend due to the level of mess. You cannot relax on a long holiday for fear of the clutter that needs your mental attention (even if you rarely do anything to practically deal with it). In any of these scenarios your clutter is in control of you as opposed to you being in charge of your living space and possessions.

The freedom to be you or to live this Lighter Life, is about having only those belongings and possessions in your home space that you need to be happy and settled. I am not referring to minimalism here, but to being aware of what you have and how to find it when you need it. The freedom to be yourself is immensely valuable. It is very much at odds with any sense of being trapped or held back by the volume of stuff which invades your private space and potentially or actually hinders your decision to think, act and choose freely about what you can do.

Your glut of possessions, and the overwhelm of thinking you have to deal daily with the clutter, is a massive drain on you emotionally as well as practically, and there is no better time to put your focus on this issue than today. If you are ever frustrated by the amount of stuff and how this might be holding you back, then you know must deal with it. The basics of you not living the life you want stem from the clutter you drag around with you.

Not happy with the cost of your home environment? Sell off enough that you can downsize to a more affordable property, or raise funds to place into savings and investments.

Take on a good part time job that will pay you regular income for your time, but put all those additional earnings into investments.

Start a side hustle for some passive income with the potential to leverage upwards.

Disappointed that you have not followed up the hobbies and activities which bring you happiness? Make space for them in your home and you will free yourself up to put the activity in your diary and make it happen. Brush the dust off that skipping rope and start to use it. Take your hobby gear out of the garage and get busy with what you love.

Fed up with your lack of social life or avoidance of good friendships? Declutter another space in your home for more good energy to replace the stagnation that has been holding you down and keeping you depressed or sad about the lack of social engagement with others. Clear a space today. It doesn't have to be a whole room. Start with a shelf or that top drawer of underwear. Maybe go through one box that has been sitting in the cupboard below your stairs.

Living this Lighter Life is not restricted to reducing the emotional and physical weight of the items in your home, though you do need to give attention to the fact that letting go of physical things does create a sense of feeling lighter about your situation in general. It gives you as well a great sense of immediacy about your decision making abilities. Where the excess of belongings in your space is creating the actual appearance of a home that is filled or cluttered or 'stuck', the opposite of this is that a reduction of those belongings brings with it the real opportunity to take advantage of the better things that will make themselves available. In preparation for our recent home move we each went through our clothes and decided what we wanted to take with us versus what we actually had in our drawers and wardrobes.

One day in a very simple process I lifted out all the shirts from my wardrobe and laid them on the bed in a pile. I had two dozen shirts on hangers. Asking myself *"Do I love this shirt and feel good when I wear it?"* I went through them in ten minutes and let go of nine. The fifteen shirts I hung back in the wardrobe are all smart, gorgeous or look great. In my chest of drawers I repeated the process and lifted out all twenty tee shirts, putting them on the bed so I could clearly see and touch each one. I repeated the process with a similar *"Do I love this tee shirt and feel good when I wear it?"* How many did I keep? Ten to keep and ten to bag for the charity shop.

In one hour I had removed the following clothes:

Nine long sleeved shirts.

Ten tee shirts.

Three pairs of shorts.

Three winter coats.

Twenty seven neck ties.

Three bed or sofa throws.

A total of fifty five items from one hour of focus. If I had looked through the items and thought to myself *"Do I like this shirt?"* or *"Is this coat nice?"* I may not have let any of them go. By putting a specific *"Do I feel good when I wear it?"* on the item I was making a much clearer, emotionally based decision. Four large bin bags went with me to the charity shop the next day and it felt great to hand them over and to understand that these clothes and the blankets could have a second life, being useful, good or comforting for another person. But when I stepped out of the goodwill store I felt amazing, I felt lighter in my own self.

This is what the Lighter Life is all about, being in the place within yourself where you are letting go of the emotional baggage that comes with all the 'stuff' that holds us back. Letting go of the physical so often brings with it a lifting of the emotional or sensed weight upon our shoulders. Much of the time we don't even know this heaviness is there, but at the moment of letting something leave our space or our ownership, we then feel the lifting of the burden we had not known we were carrying.

Meeting some people enjoying the Lighter Life.

At the very start of the year I volunteered at a countryside youth hostel for walkers and climbers, in the heart of the beautiful English Lake District. I was part of a ten person group who were there to prepare the hostel for the next six months of heavy use by visitors. We all worked together to clear rooms of furniture in advance of commercial carpet cleaners. In small teams of two and three we painted the common room and dining rooms, we painted corridors and stairwells. One day I worked outside and pushed wheelbarrows of gravel to create the paths around the campsite. On another I chopped up small branches and old timber pallets to create the kindling for the open fire in the main common room and bar area. It was a brilliant week away from home, working at practical tasks each day and then being free in the late afternoon for a walk on the mountains that surrounded us and a chat in the bar and by the log fire each evening. Each day I chatted with whoever I was paired up with for our work and it was fascinating to see a glimpse of the lighter life in action for these other volunteers.

Rob - Living with Less.

Rob had been working for the past year at a timber chalet holiday home site in Austria, ensuring that six cabins were always ready for the scheduled arrival of holiday makers. He had arrived back from Austria just a week before our working party in the Lake District. The next week he was going on to repeat the process at a hostel in Ambleside. Then again at other youth hostels in Keswick, Longthwaite, Settle, and on to York. In all he was going to be living and volunteering in eight different hostels on working parties over three months until taking up a full time job at an adventure holiday site in Scotland from March to October. Through our conversations I learned that he had only as many clothes as he needs for two weeks in between washing them. He keeps these in his car along with a laptop and half a dozen paperback books for his entertainment.

He has no home and very few possessions. The few things he regards as valuable he keeps stored at his step-mom's house. Otherwise he lives by attending working parties at hostels for three months of each year and receiving a small amount of expenses money each time. The other nine months of the year he does paid full time work at holiday sites where he receives his accommodation for free. He saves successfully because with no accommodation costs and all his food provided by the adventure camps, what can he spend money on? For two or three nights every ten days, between each volunteer week, he will either sleep in his car or stay over at a friends house, or go back to stay with his stepmother. Rob is 48 years old and has been doing this for the last ten years.

The conversation with him about not having many possessions, not owning a house, and never having owned one, was a new perspective for me and opened up some fresh ways of looking at his experience. The obvious light-bulb moment for me was the realisation that for so many regular volunteers the companionship they get while on a working holiday is the reason they are so often here.

Lisa - Van Life.

Lisa was on the same week with me. Incredibly she has spent 40 consecutive weeks living at hostels and working or volunteering to have somewhere to stay. She has a small van which she can sleep in when not working at a hostel. It is kitted out with a gas stove, a foam covered bed platform, blankets and a couple of bags of her clothing. I learn that she has a one bedroom flat in a small community on the border between England and Scotland and she goes back to this as and when she is not volunteering. By structuring her volunteering weeks on an often back to back basis, she is often away from her flat for three months at a time. Having minimal possessions in the flat she has created a lifestyle where she meets new people every week she is away. Her expense money covers all her costs of travel between hostels. Like me and the rest of us, she was fed and given good accommodation during the working week, so her savings increase steadily across the year.

Rob and Lisa were just two of the group I was with that week who have made volunteering and working, in places that provide food and accommodation, a strong part of their lighter lifestyle. Of the other seven I worked alongside, five of them all volunteered regularly and spent between six weeks and twelve weeks each year away from their own homes. So just two of the ten of us were new to this way of living lighter. Half of my new friends were single and half had a partner at home.

My week in their company was a tremendous insight

into how you can have more opportunity and greater adventure. Each of the people I spoke with about this lifestyle choice said directly to me or more casually in group conversations, that they had cut back on their possessions at home in order to be able to see a volunteer opportunity they wanted and apply for it. They knew they could lock up the house or apartment and head off to the location to enjoy themselves while contributing to a cause they believed in. In this case the creation of clean and refreshed accommodation for the walkers, climbers and runners who look to stay with like minded people when enjoying the countryside, and being able to return at dusk to such gorgeous locations and good evening company.

THREE

The emotional life of 'Stuff'

WE ARE SO CLOSELY TIED to our belongings that while we may understandably want to break free of the clutter that surrounds us, we first have to deal with the emotional issues which have stopped us from taking action. The confusion can come from you having a different emotional attachment to one item that another member of your household or a close friend will have with it. If your best friend thinks that having a dozen antique clocks in her house is normal and acceptable and you think it eccentric or even odd, you will see where I am going with this.

You might have a garage filled with walking frames, an electric powered mobility scooter that has long since eroded to being useless, and an upright piano. All these things arrived at your home twenty years ago when your grandfather died and none of your other relatives stepped up to the plate. You took responsibility for clearing these items, and for one reason or another you never managed to dispose of them. Your friend might have an attachment to the clocks because of her own family history and the ways in which she has accumulated them over several years.

What's your own story about the garage that can no longer be used for car storage or as a home workshop? In this way you see that one persons acceptable storage is seen by someone else as a pile of weird rubbish that should be chucked out. Here are some very common excuses :

1. *"This might be useful one day."*

Of course this is true to some extent, but how much do you need to bend reality to consider that you should keep 5 flathead screwdrivers of the same size, or that there should be 6 breadknives in your kitchen when one will do the same job? How about the many sleeping bags and knitted blankets in the spare bedroom? You've hung on to these since your kids were teenagers and you keep them in case you and some future visitors should be snowed in one extreme winter! It doesn't matter how you justify keeping these things, because your reasons have served you well until today. I ask you to consider them from a fresh perspective. If it might be useful, but you haven't used it in a year, let it go. Bag it, box it and take it to the goodwill shop.

There is a tendency to learn from our parents and grandparents that everything has a potential future value. We learned their value system and in most cases the good things we were taught can help us in life and we can pass on the good skills to our children and friends we care about. But there were things which were relevant forty years ago that just have no value now in a different, faster, more complicated, less self-reliant approach to life where we are these days.

Do you need to know how to build furniture in your garage, or keep all the tools to do so?

Should you be skilled in curtain making, dress making, book binding, or picture framing?

Is bike repair a skill you consider hugely valuable?

Should you hold onto all the furniture items in your home? If two of your live in your apartment or house, should you have enough seating for another dozen people?

My Mum moved from her home where she and Dad raised us all, into a nursing home where she can be better looked after than if she were living alone and subject to the dangers and worry of infirmity and falling. My brother and I calculated that in the downstairs rooms of the old family home we have three sofas, three large armchairs, eight folding garden chairs and a glass dining table, eight stacking chairs and a dining table for the sun lounge, one dining table and four chairs for the middle dining room, and two writing desks and chairs. That's enough seating for thirty four people in a house that Mum has lived in on her own for more than ten years!

The house doesn't feel cluttered, but this volume of furniture represents extreme clutter. It also serves as a reminder that where nine of us once lived together, it was in a house that hosted parties, events, prayer groups, history club meetings, parish meetings and where there was always a chair to pull up and chat with my parents. Nostalgia and clutter do tend to exist arm in arm. My brother and I will work through the furniture and see who wants want - and will turn up to collect it - and then decide where we donate the rest to ensure it continues to serve where it is needed.

2. *"I have to keep this. It was a gift".*

To which I say, *"But was it a gift you loved immediately and knew you would always treasure?"* If not, let it go. We can fill our homes with birthday presents, art work from school when our children were toddlers, wedding presents from people who had bad taste in their choice of gift, or from recent presents we were given at a family gathering. The moment something has been given to you it is up to you to choose what you do with it. Why do you see so many good quality things uploaded onto auction sites immediately after Christmas, Thanks Giving and of course throughout the year as people let go of the birthday and housewarming gifts they do not appreciate?

Keeping something you don't like in your house is a negative behaviour in that it does not truly represent who you are. Holding onto a gift when you do not like it, out of fear that you might hurt the feelings of the gift giver, is no way to lead your life as an adult. This whole process of Letting Go is about making your living space somewhere that is calm, supportive and filled with the energy you like. This means that what you have on display and see as you move around your home are items that you like and appreciate for their style, design, or attractiveness.

If Aunty Mary gave you a hideous vase as a wedding present five years or fifteen years ago, it should not be on the mantelpiece, on the shelf or even in the house. Sell,

Donate, Gift or Bin. Certainly remove it from your space. Aunty Mary will understand. The item and your feelings and thoughts about the item are not the same thing. If you love the person, but don't like the gift, let it go. Your home should be a place of calm, not of guilt or unease. This process is all about you. Put yourself and your feelings and happiness first.

3. *"That cost me a lot of money. I have to keep it."*

Guess what? Life moves on and so should you. I truly feel for you when you explain to me that once upon a time that jug or lamp cost you a lot of money on your payday. At the time it might have been a good idea because you bought something which seemed special at the time. But right now is the time zone we are dealing with, not yesterday or even yesteryear. Does that jug get used? Do you fill it with flowers every week? In the warm days of summer picnics is it filled with water and ice for family gatherings? If the answer is 'no', then it's time to go! Remember the mantra now - S. D. G. B. Remember what this means - Sell, Donate, Gift or Bin.

Money is important. We all need it to live with and we have to make our way in the world using money to pay our bills and buy our food and utilities. But the life you are paying for is the same life that might just contain a bit of clutter. Am I right? So use your money wisely, make it work well for the downshift lifestyle that you want to create for yourselves. Money is also a very emotional topic and it provokes reaction in every one of us. The economy in many places right now is in a mess. If we are honest, we could all do with an extra income and this is reflected in the growth of people being willing to chat about having a side business or a side hustle to add to what they earn from a job or from self-employed work that keeps them busy.

No one will judge you for being cautious about what you spend your money on, but why hang onto something that has more realisable value once sold and gone that it had while sitting in your home and adding no value. Keeping the thing in your house will not bring back the money you spent to acquire it. The money left your wallet the day you bought it. Time has moved on and maybe the use or value of the item has changed too.

We once had a neighbour who had three cars on his drive. None of them worked. All had flat tyres and rusted bodywork. That's his choice. But one day he might want to move house and sell up. He will have to pay for someone to take the junk off his drive, but in the meantime the whole place will look unattractive and every time he looks out of his kitchen window he must be thinking *"What have I done storing that junk in my space?"* It can't possibly bring him any positive thoughts about the hanging on to clutter that he has gone through. If it doesn't add value, joy or pleasure to you life, let it go. If it has no value, is broken, does not support your lifestyle, let it go.

If you want to really feel the pain of money spent just consider the cost of holding the things you still have but which you do not need. In cost of rent or mortgage that you pay monthly there is a direct and measurable link between the cost of your clutter and the money going out each month. If your house is twenty percent clutter, then the cost of that clutter equates to twenty percent of your accommodation cost. The same is true of your insurance each month. I hope that motivates you to take action. You are paying to insure this rubbish! Stop it now.

You and I have both made mistakes with what we have bought in the past and how we have used or misused our funds. It's time to forgive ourselves for these errors and to accept that an item, which we once appreciated enough to pay a lot for, no longer holds that status or value and can be let go of. You did the best you could with what you had at the time. You really did think you were making a good decision when you bought that item. I know. Grasping hold of this will allow you to move forward and say goodbye to the item without anymore guilt.

4. *"I was chasing my dreams with this."*

There are some items we hold onto because they strongly represent our goals and dreams. Some of these we were chasing and then gave up or perhaps simply changed direction. Others we feel are an important part of our life right now and we still consider that we are pursuing that goal in our actions every week. These are items which the emotional attachment makes very difficult to let go of. Sports trophies from when we were at our physical peak, framed team pictures from another life, motivational posters from a business we were a part of, or painting supplies and blank canvases we thought we would have used by now in developing our skills and hobbies to a better level.

We struggle to let go of these because it feels brutal and painful to face the fact that we didn't achieve this goal or that dream. We feel like we messed up or we broke the promise we made to ourselves. I relate to this a lot. I have USB sticks of unfinished manuscripts. I have the bronze and silver award for a prestigious young person programme we have in our country, but never managed to finish it and earn the gold award. That is something I have regretted for years, and I remind myself how much pleasure it was to achieve the first two awards and the good things I did to accomplish these levels. We had community service projects, volunteer activities, expeditions in the countryside and camping trips where we learned map reading, teamwork and survival skills. These were very positive times in my teenage years and I loved the activity, teamwork, the leadership and guidance we received and think fondly of these times.

Connecting with the emotions of this theme of letting go of previously aspirational clutter can help you to become free of the feelings we associate with not completing goals. Put these thoughts to bed and look now to find new goals and opportunities where you wisdom and enhanced skills will give you an advantage and allow you to start strong with what you have. When you discard the things which represented old aspirations you have not failed at those. You instead need to be gentle with yourself and recognise the goals and points of focus for the life you lead today.

Letting go of unfinished projects, discarding items that you have been unconsciously aware of not completing, and clearing out old resources you will never use to help you with your current goals, this can be immensely satisfying and liberating. Forgive yourself for not accomplishing what you had once been convinced you were going to do. Letting go of these old aspirations, for something that has probably not been a part of your life for some years, will free you up for new and inspiring opportunities and activities. This is where your focus needs to be, on your current goals and aspirations. These are the ones that matter right now.

5. *"I feel sentimental about this. I have to keep it."*

Of all the areas of clutter reduction, letting go and facing the stuff we accumulate, it is the sentimental attachment to things that presents the biggest challenge to discarding, and that's why I have kept this section of the theme until last. So many approaches to hoarding, decluttering, letting go and to dealing with the mess in our homes are rational in their style. But we are not rational creatures, we are human beings. Better put we are 'humans being'. That means we are all emotional, that we attribute meaning to almost everything we do, see and to all of our actions around the topic of decluttering.

So every item in the home has some form of emotional attachment for us. It could be a pencil, a shirt, a saucepan, a pair of shoes or a box of toys. The single biggest obstacle to us making a good job of dealing with the stuff we have accumulated is the sentimental obstacle. We may feel we have to climb over it, step around it, or crawl underneath it, but deal with it we must if we are to make progress in any way at all. Every object in your house can have some emotional pull on you, normally associated with a memory or an image in your head about when you acquired it, who gave it to you, how you were feeling when you bought it. Each of these feelings, memories and reminiscences take up so much space in your head. Sometimes I am amazed I get anything done for all the things in my mind! These are all competing for your attention and there is only so much time you have to deal with each thought or emotional response.

Touch everything.

When deciding to deal with the clutter that surrounds you and which overwhelms or drags you down emotionally, you are going to have to be tough with yourself. The decisions you make about what goes and what stays will be hard ones a lot of the time. But once made they should put you in a better place emotionally. In order to get results that last and which make a difference in your home environment, if you pick up every item and handle it, you then have to make a choice over what to do with it.

The action of touching each thing strengthens your emotional connection to the decluttering process. You might be telling yourself that you have to keep something for sentimental reasons, but what are they? Could you justify them to a friend? If the thing you hold cannot be placed on display in your home, lose it. If the item is not worth keeping in a readily accessible part of your house, and I do not mean a box in the basement or a bag in the attic, it has to go. Your task is to keep things which bring value or happiness, which support the life your choose or which should accompany you on the downshift lifestyle you seek. If everything has emotion attached to it, then you are going to keep only those items which are imbued with good, special and treasured feelings.

Keep a journal.

As with every day in which you are discarding things from your home space, be aware of how you feel as you let go of them. Be mindful of the emotions you associate with a selection of items, or the box you fill with things for the goodwill. Continue to be grateful for your observations and, if it helps to note them down, get them captured and summarised in your journal. You may let go of the items, but you will still have access to the way you felt about the process and it takes up virtually no space to store your thoughts on some special pages. You can keep the simple journal in place of the much larger volumes of stuff you are now able to let go of.

When you want to move closer to the significance of some of the objects in your home and discover the real emotional connection you have to each piece, here are some simple techniques that may be useful.

Create a virtual memory Box.

Take digital pictures of many of the items which you have struggled with holding onto. Either you want to have them in your home space or your don't. It really is this simple in reality. In practice however, we know that life does not exist in a purely black and white, binary way. Save images of the things you like, but which you would not willingly go out and buy again. The pictures are things you can always go back to if you have that sense of nostalgia for the item.

Let Heirlooms move within Your Family.

Just because you don't want to hang on to your Uncle Bob's massively heavy two volume collection of The 1938 World Encyclopaedia doesn't mean that you have to throw this away or wait for a few months for it to be listed and sold via an online auction platform. Put the word around that you have this to go to a good home and you might discover a cousin who would love it, with or without any pre-existing good memories of Uncle Bob. One of my great grandpas was a regimental sergeant major in the Guards. It never occurred to me that someone else in a different branch of the family might be interested in his medals and shooting trophies which came to me via my Dad, until I realised in my forties that I had a cousin who had great grandpas's parade ground Swagger Stick and that we shared some old sepia pictures of grandpa in common with one another. It was nice to connect and look at the family history side of things from our different perspectives.

Let Go of Gifts that Get You Down.

A gift is given freely or shouldn't be given at all. Where it feels like a weight around your shoulders, let it go as soon as you can, without reservation or doubt over letting it go. Have your house be a place of peace and joy by ensuring that the things you didn't choose are still in line with your values and visions about your world. If you feel awkward about it, let it go.

Choose what is a 'Keeper'.

Hang on to the crazy, the cool, the beautiful and the items that are evocative of good times and which give you that same sense or feeling when you look at them or hold them in your hands and visualise the good times they represent.

Create a Scrapbook.

Take family pictures from your childhood, or the life of your parents and grandparents. This way you don't have to hang onto hundreds of images, but can find a few dozen pictures, along with marriage certificates, holiday postcards, travel tickets and school reports, to create something which can be cherished and which will trigger plenty of good thoughts on its own.

Let the Item have a New Life.

If you decide that the piece is good enough for someone other than yourself to cherish, give thought to where it might be better placed. This could be with a family member, friend or someone whom you know would appreciate it and give it a good home. The item could help them set up home, downsize when they are starting over or simply be a gift they would appreciate to cheer up an aspect of their dwelling.

Recycle, Reuse, Remodel.

Some things you love are gorgeous, but bulky. A jacket, an heirloom blanket, a wedding dress, a uniform no longer worn. You can create some special keepsake pieces with these, and choose to do the cutting and stitching yourself or take them to a specialist tailor or dress maker and seek their help and involvement in making a new item that serves to remind you of the positive experiences, memories and good times you associate with the items that no longer need to take up so much space. Bed throws, quilts and scatter cushion covers come to mind as potential remakes of the originally larger items which can be repurposed. An old piano can be repurposed as a drinks cabinet. A pedal operated sewing machine table can find new life as a desk or eye catching curio stand. A stone or diamond from a ring that is not your style, can be extracted and reset into a piece of jewellery that delights you.

Mortality and More.

When my Grandpa on my Mum's side bought himself a writing desk, a bureau to be more accurate, it was 1927 and he was not yet married. So much of his life was ahead of him. He had not met my grandmother. Fast forward ninety plus years and I have that bureau as my own writing desk now. I never met John Harris. But his widow was my Grandma Alice and I loved visiting her. When she passed away the desk came to my Mum, and as a preschooler I was fascinated by the closing front cover and it's hinges, by the spiral turned legs. I loved the little felt lined drawers and the leather cover of the desk. The smell of the bottles of ink and the balance of the pens inside it all drew my attention. During my senior school years I did my homework on the leather top surface of the opened bureau. This piece of furniture has lived in four houses and served several generations of our family. Previous owners are long since dead and buried and I think sometimes about what will happen to this piece of furniture going forward with my own demise. Will one of my sons want it for their own place? He doesn't need it while he is at university. He may not have space for it in his first home. He might just not want it.

You see the problem here in this simple example of a piece of wooden furniture that has so much more history now than when a young bachelor called John Harris bought it simply because he liked it. We complicate an inanimate object by giving it meaning, by wrapping it with the history we know and the memories we imagine and part recall. We imbue these possessions with those same magical qualities which I have written of elsewhere and which we gather about us.

We do this because we are human and to make sense of the world around us we have to give meaning or significance to everything we see or do. Every small ornament, trinket, or medallion. Each item of clothing or piece of furniture. To everything we add a story. It is how we cope with so much in our lives, to differentiate one thing or experience from another potentially similar item or event. It is precisely because of this attaching of meaning, memory and significance that we find such struggle in letting go of many of the items we have in our homes.

Find ways to identify the stories and the emotions that form some part of your nostalgic connection to your belongings. If you can encapsulate these into your journal and into the photos you take and share, you will find it so much easier to let go of what no longer needs you to hold on to it. By letting something go you allow it a new life and a fresh purpose elsewhere.

FOUR

Where do I start?

YOU HAVE THOUGHT ABOUT THIS, sat with your head in your hands and worried about the clutter, the chaos and the mess. To say nothing of the overwhelm, stress and constant drain on your energy. Now it's time to begin the process of working through the things you have around you and to actually let some of them go. I feel your pain, really I do.

Grab your journal and take the time to note how you are feeling right now. Limit this to thirty minutes or however long it takes you to enjoy a coffee with your pen and notebook!

Be honest about how you feel approaching the project of removing this junk and clutter from your home. If you are scared then write about this to yourself. What is most worrying for you? Are there some aspects making you feel nervous or jittery? Stick with a pre chosen time limit for the journalling activity and use this to get your thoughts and feelings down on paper. We don't want you to be so absorbed in your notes that you never get around to the work of discarding!

Picture your starting point.

After journalling about the emotional place you are in as you begin the declutter, I am going to ask you to do one thing that will take just minutes out of your day, but which will have a powerful benefit. Grab your cell phone and take pictures of every single room in the house. Stand at each doorway and take a picture of the room in front of you. Then go to an opposite side or corner of the room and take some other pictures looking back towards the doorway. As you build your photo album of the room, make sure you have an image of each area captured and stored on your phone. Do this with your living area, dining space, sleeping area. But also do the bathrooms and the kitchen. Take photos of your kitchen with every cupboard open. Take a picture of that random dumping ground under the sink. Open your bathroom cabinets and capture an image of the contents. I dare you to!

If you have a garage, a basement or an attic, make sure to gather images of each of these areas so you are fully aware of what you are dealing with, but also to have an accurate starting position from where you are approaching the whole task of decluttering. For many people this is a harrowing process because it gives you the evidence of how out of control you have become with the operation of your home as a space where you gather, hoard, store and accumulate quite so much. I promise you though, that some time from now you will look at the before and after pictures and feel such a sense of pride and accomplishment, you will be wanting to show everyone the results you have achieved and the completely different space you have created through your own effort, dedication and focus.

With the picture album recorded, you need to start with a section of your home that you can manage to deal with in one go. Here I don't mean a whole room though. You need to be realistic and also kind to yourself. You want an early win so that you will come back and do more. This can be a drawer in a desk, a shelf in your living room or that cupboard under the stairs. When you are starting out to begin the battle of clearing your clutter you need to give yourself an early victory so you will stay with the process tomorrow and the next day. There are plenty of TV programmes or articles out there which promote the instant makeover of your living space. From looking at these it seems they are all about removing items from one room so that the room is left looking great with so much less in it after your work. Of course, this doesn't deal with the corridors and other rooms where you have dragged and dumped the items you removed.

With our own declutter process in preparation for moving to a smaller living space we started with weekend sessions where we could focus on what we wanted to do. Every Saturday morning for two months we opened drawers, unwrapped sealed boxes in the garage, moved cases of luggage to see what was inside the bags and then realised how much junk we were stacking and storing for no useful reason. The first time we tried this an hour was enough to send us into a head-spin, concerned to realise just how much we had and scared that we had no process for dealing with it. We had a garage filled from floor to ceiling, an external thirty foot corridor that ran down the outside of the house and which was sealed from bad weather by a corrugated plastic roof. This long space was filled with magazines, some old bikes, kids car seats, a fridge unit, used cupboards, several chests of drawers and two dozen stacked plastic crates that I had not looked inside for six years.

That first hour gave us an insight into the scale of the job and we retreated back into the house with a headache! We started closer to home and went through our clothing drawers in the bedroom. We each pulled out one of our own drawers at a time and started with underwear and tee shirts. I learned that I had some tatty underwear and more than a dozen single socks without their matching partner. These all went into a bin bag. Then I paired all the socks and folded them into smaller bundles, easy to find and store in an orderly way. I did the same with my underwear, throwing half away and leaving space to buy some new items. After one hour I was smiling broadly at the beauty that was now represented by my first two drawers. Later that day I achieved the same with a drawer of tee shirts. I never knew I owned twenty tee shirts, but once they had each been folded to a uniform standard, the drawer only seemed half filled and I could now see every shirt by colour. Again, this is about making things easy for you.

The next weekend I tackled my wardrobe and identified that I had twenty seven long sleeve worksheets and fifteen casual shirts. Eight woolen sweaters in three warm colours and seven sweatshirts or hoodies just in blue or grey. Three autumn jackets, three elegant and expensive raincoats (none of which I had worn in five years. Who knew? I was horrified that I had so much and that I wore so little of it. To know this about your wardrobe will be a revelation because you are unconscious about the state of your wardrobe.

So just start with something simple like your bedroom clothing drawers, or a wardrobe. This allows you to have an early win and gives you an insight into what you already have versus what you need. Knowing the difference between these gives you the scope to let go of a lot of unneeded items and will give you such a positive feeling about what you have achieved.

Set time aside to Achieve your Declutter Goal.

You have come this far with occasional peaks and troughs of clutter activity. For one month you let the mess build up and the next month you run about tidying, hiding, throwing away or storing things in a different room from the one that hurts your eyes when you look around. Just as this approach won't work for you in the long term, attempting to properly deal with your clutter for a few hours every few months and thinking this will get you great results, this is short sighted.

You must set several hours aside each week or allocate time every day for a month and commit to this in your diary. Bring your diary up to speed and block out time when you can allocate at least an hour to the process each day for the next week. Put the appointment with yourself in the diary because you have to make this happen. Understand the truth of this process, that it is going to take hard work, both in terms of the practical effort, but also emotionally. You have committed yourself to looking at and working your way through the tonne of stuff you have spent years accumulating, and which you are going to let go of in a matter of weeks or perhaps just two months at most.

This is a big mental task. Creating a schedule for the declutter work, you are committing to getting yourself out of this messy and chaotic place where you have lost yourself. This is enough to get you results that lift your mood and give you daily victories. These results will ensure you commit to the same hours invested in the next week. Once it becomes a habit for you it will become enjoyable and bring the obvious benefits of your endeavours. Repeating this day after day for a month will see your home looking like a brand new place, with fresh energy released right across the space.

Each time you successfully have that declutter appointment with yourself, you are reinforcing the commitment to getting this done. Every single item that leaves your house and which is not replaced, means you have successfully regained territory in your own living space. You are building up a new behaviour of dealing consciously with each item in your home and the role it has in your environment. Celebrate the results by looking at the before and after pictures of your home. The comparison images will shock you and delight you too. You are winning at this.

Challenge Yourself to get Specific Results.

List the number of rooms in your house and then rank them by how much they annoy or frustrate you by the level of clutter within each room. This is now your map of what to tackle and how much time you may need to allocate to each room. The least cluttered room might be the room that you allocate as a Holding Space for moving things to before you then remove them from that space and out into the world beyond your front door. Do you remember the outside corridor space I told you about? This became our holding space for all things considered clutter.

Everything was matched to a different pile marked Sell, Donate, Gift or Bin. Set some goals as you move around your home. Do you think that your wardrobes might generate six boxes of clutter to be removed? How does this compare with the kitchen cupboards and storage units? Are these another six or will you reduce your estimate to four boxes of clutter or surplus items to be removed and let go of. What about the junk in your study or in the basement where you have a tendency to dump things and forget about them? Be prepared for big numbers when you look at the rooms where you have your wardrobes, shoes, seasonal clothing and holiday gear.

What I thought would be a four box process for my

own wardrobe ended up being twice that when I accounted for footwear, sweatshirts, coats and jackets! Again, you don't have to keep count, but here's why it seems to help a lot of people. We are human beings driven by accomplishment. We measure things by value, volume, amount and quantity. We don't just live in an apartment or a house. Instead we opt for a two bedroom apartment or a three bedroom house. So when it comes to you tackling your home clutter and liberating new space, to looking at whether you will stay in that newly decluttered home or choosing to enjoy a downsized lifestyle, then you will find it useful to keep score as you move through the challenge you have set yourself. By measuring and counting your clutter, you will know the progress you are making.

First, Clear the Decks!

A small Waste Bin is often enough to get started. The faster you fill it with things the easier it seems to raise your levels of excitement and accomplishment. You can even get the same dopamine rush to your senses when throwing things away that you once got when you bought items you didn't need! How strange is that?

Take a drawer out of a cabinet in your living room or in your kitchen and go through it. Let's take that kitchen example. There will be at least one drawer in your kitchen that sometimes you struggle to close. Am I right? This is where you begin. Empty the drawer onto a work surface and work through each item.

Ask yourself:

Do I need this?

How many of these utensils do I have versus how many do I need?

If two of you live together in the house and you have twenty knives and forks, twelve desert spoons and twenty tea spoons, surely half of these can go?

If you have six wooden spoons, four spatulas, five breadknives, and three soup ladles, do you think you might be able to reduce each of these to just two.

How about your mug collection? When we started on this journey we counted twenty seven mugs in two sections of our kitchen, for just two of us! It was genuinely an emotional struggle, I kid you not, but we managed to get this down to just twelve mugs. We kept the most beautiful and some that matched. I took the surplus mugs into work and distributed them among our tenants. Several institutions in your neighbourhood who work to help people move from hostel accommodation to independent living would love to get a box of utensils, crockery and cutlery, pots and pans.

You get the message by now and can do the same throughout your kitchen with each drawer and cupboard section. Don't even get me started on cups and saucers that are held back to be used 'for special'! Two boxes of tissue wrapped cups and saucers were in our outer corridor for just such special occasions and we realised we had only opened the boxes and used the contents just one time in two years for an event where we had about sixty friends round for a fund raising garden party opened by the town Mayor. By taking 'Lack of Use' as a new category for sorting these items we were able to send two dozen sets to a charity shop where they will have raised an extra $100 and more by selling them off one set at a time. Tea towels were jammed into a kitchen drawer which we struggled to close. We counted thirty one. In a house for two people this is just ridiculous! We kept eight and let the rest go.

Tidy Up with a Waste Bin!

You have the Waste Bin to hand and you move around one room with it. Look for the items that have randomly landed on the surfaces of this room. A bottle opener, a cigarette lighter, a pad of paper and three pens. A set of car keys and some coins. A document you brought home from work and read one evening, before abandoning it on the arm of the sofa instead of putting it back in your work bag. An empty card box from a light bulb you changed two days ago. A local newspaper that came in the mail. Some empty envelopes from post you have read through, plus the utility bill and local tax letter that both need filing. All of these items go in the waste bin and you move around the house with it for ten minutes to put each item where it belongs.

The bottle opener goes in a kitchen drawer, and the paper envelopes and junk mail go into the recycling bin in the same kitchen. The car keys go into a tray in the hall and the coins into a jar on a bookshelf. The cigarette lighter, paper pad, pens and the work document go into your work bag in the hall. The utility bill and the local tax letter get hole punched and filed in the section of the home binder where they belong, on top of the previous ones so you can find the most recent first. This simple waste bin exercise is one you can use every day to ensure that the things you keep get back to where they belong in your home. But this is not dealing with the real clutter. For this you need some bigger tools!

The Big Box Approach.

Simply put, you repeat what you did with the Waste Bin, but now you are tackling the surplus, the extra, the actual junk, the items that are not for recycling or filing, but which take up so much more space and energy in your home. Grab that list you made of the rooms in your house and which you had ranked by severity of clutter. Take your Big Box or Crate into that room and fill it with anything on the floor, with things on a shelf unit or in a cupboard. Today, for the hour you have set aside for this, fill the box once, twice or three times. As soon as it is full take it into that least cluttered room where you have created a designated space for things that you will be sorting.

Remember that you have categorised these already to be : Sell, Donate, Gift or Bin and empty your Big Box in line with these categories of clutter. You are placing things into each of these piles until there is enough of a load to move away from your home. Everything else is straight for the bin. The key to winning at this stage is that you do what it says on each grouping of items. Don't let yourself be distracted.

A word of guidance for the unsure or the weak hearted. If it doesn't fit into one of those four criteria, you are keeping it and that's OK. You are letting it stay where it is because you love it or it brings such happiness to your life when you see it. I hope that stops the panic for some of you. This is your stuff and you can keep the best of it. You are getting rid of the clutter, the waste, the surplus and the junk. Stay calm and get busy decluttering!

SELL

This can be a task the whole household gets behind and if so, you get to share the rewards from the selling activity. If you want to motivate a teenager, you may have just found a good way forward! Get them involved in listing the items for sale in online platforms. Reward them with seeing the progress made and the additional cash that comes in from the successful sale of items that they list.

There are several ways you can move on this task of determining which items get to be sold on. The Big Box is moved around the house during each of your allocated and time-bound decluttering sessions and it gets to the place where you sort into the four categories of Sell, Donate, Gift or Bin. The selling activity can happen in a variety of ways. Any one of many online auction sites can be used to advertise what you have for sale. A silk tie that cost you $50 new can reach $20 when advertised online. Three or four pictures uploaded from your cell phone and a short description will see it sold within the month, and you have $20 bucks to add to your holiday fund or family treat fund. This two lamp bases that are made from beautifully turned wood are sold for $40 the pair plus postage. The vintage 1940's story books, hard-bound and with gorgeous illustrations under tissue sell for $15 per book and you had been hoarding forty of them. You can hold out for slow and steady sales over a month or more, or you take an offer of $300 for the lot. It all goes into the fund.

Bigger items are not so ripe for online sale and sending by mail. Instead consider using an online marketplace listing where you get to list the pictures of that polished wood dining table and four chairs, or the spare desk or the two armchairs that have been in your garage for a year. You click and upload the pics, and the next day some buyers come for the separate items and you pocket $60 cash for the table and chairs, $50 for the desk and another $50 for the two big armchairs. That's another $160 for the holiday fund or which you can split between debt reduction and treats for the household. But you have cleared a volume of stuff from your house and put money in the bank at the same time.

A word of warning here for the cautious. In the process of finding things you are happy to sell you might get the bug for online auction activity and be tempted to buy more stuff with the belief that you can bring it home to then seek to resell. Be careful and get rid of all your own clutter first!

DONATE

You take the items that end up here, down to the good-will shop as soon as you have enough to fill a couple of boxes which you can put in the car and deliver to the store next time you are in town. Every card box or black bin bag you fill with lampshades, unwanted clothes, laundered bedsheets and duvet sets, books in good reading condition or jiffy bags of unused pens and pencils, each of these has a value to your local preferred charity. You are taking stagnant energy in the form of the stuff you no longer need or want and transferring that to a place where it can be sold on and gather new energy in the form of cash money for the cause they promote and support through their work. If you are a person who likes to keep score of such activity consider the value of your gift each time you pull up out side the store with your goodies.

GIFT

This is about some of the choicer stuff you come across when rooting around in your garage, attic or den. Perhaps you will find some emotional gold deep within those wardrobes where you haven't looked behind the coats for years! You will inevitably come across things that you have held onto as family heir-loom items, and which you have enjoyed having with you over several years. Now might well be a good time to let them have a new home, still within the family. Before my Dad died he had already given me some of the beautiful things he had treasured. A velvet lined, mahogany box stored his Lewis Men chess set which he had made. My youngest son is the chess player now and so this is marked for him. A folding wooden writing desk from the Officer's Cabin of 1940's British troop ship is something Dad bought in his one of his antique hunting trips. It is gorgeous, has a secret drawer, the cut glass ink pot, has the original ship's movement document attached and also comes with research into the history of the ship, HMS Somersetshire. This is a beautiful piece of history that also looks gorgeous when kept on display in a living room and so I happily gifted this to another family member as a reminder of our Dad.

What have you got that you are happy to let go of, knowing it can have a renewal of life in a fresh setting, where it will be loved and appreciated? It has already served you well and brought you pleasure. You have the memories of it in your life and can take several digital pictures of it before handing it over to the next person who will appreciate it. I think of these as Legacy Treasures or Legacy Gifts. Other items you have which are simply in good order can be used by others who will be grateful to you for the gift and able to make use of the item now that you no longer have need of it.

It doesn't have to be something of great financial value but it might have the qualities or practical function they need. A food processor, a well equipped tool box, a car jack or tyre pump. A mountain bike in good order. A collection of novels. Some electrical extension cables. Unwanted surplus furniture. A gift can be anything that you have had good use from and which still has life in it to be of use to another person or household. Let the items go and notice how different your space feels for the new energy it has within it. Write about how you feel as you let these things go into their new life somewhere else.

BIN

This is an easy one. The sooner something moves from the Bin pile to the large waste bins outside your home the better. A good and realistic goal here is that whatever you place in this pile, it does not stay here overnight, but goes outside into the designated private or communal bin areas for your home. The items here can sometimes be split between recycling and rubbish. For example, a broken wooden chair is rubbish, but the material can be recycled by your local authority as they work through waste. The same is true of glass vases, and the piles of hoarded newspapers, magazines and newsletters that you can put to recycling rather than pure rubbish which simply goes to landfill.

FIVE

Your magical things

WE STRUGGLE to let go of the items in our homes because we chose to bring them in for a reason. We love them or have given them a cherished value. We saw them as being our link to someone we have loved. Perhaps we received them from a favourite grandparent or a school teacher who was our coach and mentor. Possibly we hold onto that blanket because it was on our Aunt's bed or in a blanket box that our grandmother left to us in her will. Those vinyl records can't be played on any digital device you own in your apartment, but you hang on to the albums because of what? Your Dad had albums of his own when he was a boy so you bought your own collection of them at a car boot or flea market after hearing your Dad rave about the magic of listening on a record player. It is this magic which we often add to objects that forces us then to continue holding onto them long after any real functional or practical value has passed us by.

And this is the real reason we hang onto things,

because we are people with emotions and feelings and we assign value and meaning to everything we see or come into contact with. We have to do this to stop ourselves getting into total overwhelm or melt down when faced with a thousand and one choices every day. You see a mahogany box that your uncle stored his love letters in from your aunty before she died and so you give that simple wooden box a value in your mind. You add to it all the memories of riding a bike from your own house as a kid to see your aunty Mabel and uncle Jack. You think of all the ice creams they bought you and some of the birthday presents for your first teenage birthday. All of this heavy emotional baggage attaches itself to the box.

Now the box is not simply a 'box'. It has become a store of memory, a reflection of your childhood, a visual link to how you grew up and what you learned from good adult role models. It is so much more than wood and the pins that hold it together or the varnish that allows it to shine, or the crack in the back where it was once dropped on a pavement when your uncle moved into his care home as an elderly man. It has become a part of you. And you wonder why you find it hard to let go of the things in your life? Everything has meaning and connection - good or bad - because we give such qualities and meanings to each thing we handle. You have my understanding and my empathy with this difficult process.

Your home is a reflection of you. Your values, your sense of identity, or who you are to yourself as well as to those whose opinion you take on board. Your house or apartment is a mirror of how you feel about yourself and how you see yourself. The furniture, artwork, decorative style, clothing, photographs on display, all of these are elements of you.

Your Clothes.

A shirt you wore on your wedding day, the suit you wore on the evening you met your wife, the wedding dress from that special day twelve years ago and which is still in the wardrobe. How about those boots you wore when climbing a 3,000 foot peak ten years ago, but which haven't been worn much in recent years. The graduation gown that you wore once thirty years ago. The twenty seven ties in your wardrobe when you are not required to wear one in the workplace and only attend a handful of events each year where a suit and tie are appropriate.

Your Family Souvenirs.

The piano that had pride of place in your grandmother's living room, but which you cannot play and which takes up so much place. The walking stick and row of medals that were your grandfather's. The swivel leather chair and footstool that your Dad bought the week of his retirement in a colour you don't really like. The pocket watch that was worn by your great grandfather. The clutch bag that belonged to your mother. The pottery vase or cut glass crystal decanter that you don't use because you choose not to have flowers in the house or to serve drinks in a formal way. A photo album from a wedding one hundred years ago and which you know is somehow connected to a relative, but you don't know which one. A fountain pen that your Mum had when a school girl and which works fine, but you rarely write letters by hand. These are sometimes heirloom items which connect us to the larger family network and discarding them creates feelings of disloyalty.

Celebrity or Newsworthy Memorabilia.

A framed photo signed by a famous football star, or novels that have been dedicated by the author to yourself. That autograph book which you carried with you as a teenager to shows and music festivals for signatures of the actors or bands that you loved. Some people collect the clothing of film stars or even their cars. Some collect religious artefacts attributed to a saint or religious leader, or items recovered from tragic events like an air crash, shipwreck or military campaign.

Gift Items.

A deluxe kitchen gadget you have only used a handful of times since it was given to you as a wedding gift or home warming present eight years ago. A framed picture of a country scene you really don't like, but which is on a bedroom wall because you were given it by your Great Aunt who you loved when you were younger, but who now you can't tolerate for her crankiness. She doesn't visit, but your parents do and they might comment critically if they didn't see the picture. When people spend money on a gift for us we can get in to all sorts of guilt where we don't like or appreciate the item they bought for us. How we see our relationship to them as the gift giver can affect the way we deal with the gift.

It was just a gift, not a contract! We still allocate strong emotions to gifts we don't appreciate, especially where there is a chance the giver might enquire about our use of the gift at some future date, or at least where we think they will! The gift category of items we have among our clutter often presents some of the biggest emotional tussles when we try to let them go.

Comfort Objects from Childhood.

How about the soft toys you had as a youngster or the comfort blanket you had first in your cot and then in your bed? A book collection that was relevant to you as a six year old, but you are now twenty seven! Printed class photographs from your first year at school. A plastic crate of boxed games and toys that you might be keeping handy for your grandchildren, who are not born yet! A uniform or handbook from the scout group you were part of when you were ten and eleven, but which was three decades ago. A wooden baseball or cricket bat from teenage years when we played well at senior school level, but which is now just gathering dust in the garage.

In collecting items of value or which you attribute a value to - whether this is still holding each version of the iPhones you have owned, or having three dozen boxes of trainers dominating your bedroom cupboard - what are you achieving? You are filling your home space with stuff you do not need or use and which has been superseded by the latest phone or the newest trainers. We put the image of us as a fashionable, technical innovator on to the phones. You see yourself as a sporting woman with the boxes of trainers. You can only use one cell phone at a time. You can only run in one pair of trainers during the race or wear one pair of sneakers to the shops. But the belongings we fix around us are simply a reflection of the magical attributes we allocate to them.

We want to be special. We want to be seen as fit and strong or as techno savvy and bright. The walls of books might make us look smart and well read. The original art work on our walls will add to our creative identity and some of it might just rub off onto us. So we justify that ownership of item A, or item B, will give us the qualities we aspire to having. You could take great pictures of the medals or the jewellery and instead deposit $5,000 in the bank for your own future, but you don't. We can't manage this unless we get a real look into what we are hanging on to such things for and understanding emotionally why we do this.

We can potentially put ourselves into debt, or we reduce the potential value of our savings, in direct proportion to our desire to accumulate stuff to hide our own inhibitions or feelings of insecurity. More often than not these feelings are about not knowing our own potential, or of knowing it but not stepping up to the plate and designing the life that reflects our real self as opposed to the imagined self that we think others should see.

So much of this book and the ideas and messages within it are to help you look at the life you have versus the life you could have, to consider the happiness and satisfaction you have right now compared to the joy and contentment you could have with less stuff holding you back or tying you down. Make no mistake about this, by allocating such magical qualities to items in your home that other people would observe politely as clutter, or worse as junk, you are blocking yourself from living a higher energy, more focussed life where your distractions are reduced.

We don't set out to acquire rooms of stuff that we make little use of. Instead we attribute value to something because of the memory trigger it gives and the feelings it stirs within us. We allow this magical quality to settle on it and we end up struggling to know what to let go of because everything becomes special. All that we choose to keep has a powerful hold over us.

It need not be this way and I want to give you some simple indicators of the magical qualities you have attributed to your stuff. Use this as a helpful guide to determine what you must keep and what you can confidently discard. Making a decision about such items and their role in your thoughts and emotions, as well as in the practical tasks you carry out every day or week, will make it easier for you to let go of so much. By doing this you will allow a much lighter, more positive energy into your living space and change the focus of your life. Rather than be a guardian or custodian of hundreds of individual pieces of stuff that constantly require your attention, and drain your energy and focus, you can learn to let go of vast amounts of these. This allows you to feel more free and to live a life on purpose.

Some Indicators of potential Magical Value attributed to your objects :

If it was broken or lost would you be unhappy?

Are you reluctant to throw it away, even after you have stopped using it?

If someone took it away would you buy it back regardless of the cost?

Do you think that it could not be replaced by another of equal function or value?

Do you refer to it by name or give it a personality within your home?

Would you struggle to let it go even if someone offered you full market value?

SIX

Discarding your financial clutter

MUCH OF WHAT we view as mess are the large physical items that we can see the need to let go of. Financial clutter is less obvious to the eye and something that shows up perhaps in a series of folders, or envelopes that have been opened and perhaps not worked through. Often our actual banking arrangements can be without order and difficult to navigate.

How many bank accounts do you have, versus how many do you use regularly?

What level of service do you receive from your bank as opposed to the service you want?

How many dormant savings accounts or money passbooks do you have around the house?

Are all your paper bank statements in one place and easy to access in just five minutes?

As you look at the way you manage and monitor your finances ask yourself whether you could do this better and find the information you need faster than the time it currently takes you to locate the statements, dividends, savings records, pension information and tax payment records. The chances are high that you don't keep all your financial information in one place, that as new paperwork comes in to your home it does not systematically end up in the same place that you keep and store your financial records. This is simple to change, and requires only that you become conscious of it. Resolve this quickly and simply by keeping all financial records, statements and passbooks in the same location in your home.

Start with your Bank Statement.

Look at all the transactions for a two month period and particularly at the regular and committed payment arrangements you have set up. Are any of these for Shopping Clubs you no longer participate in, for incentive and Discount Clubs where you joined to save money and yet never have enough money to spend to qualify for the Sports and Leisure or Dining Club activities you were seduced by to begin with. If you find any of these regular payment programmes, cancel the payment and cancel the commitment. Just three or four such items at $10 to $20 a month will save you $300 - $400 and more this year. Keep that money in your account and get the potential benefit of being able to ask for a discount the next time you are going to buy something significant and have the cash available for the barter.

Can you see some transactions on your statement that you don't recognise? If so, raise the items with your bank and have them check for fraud or for some form of false transaction. Identity theft and false transactions are increasing as fraudsters become more skilled at making tiny deductions to accounts, on the correct idea that most people only query large deductions they don't recognise.

Are there regular small purchases such as Coffee and Snack Food on the way to and from work each day which might constitute $10 or $20 per day but which can add up to several thousand spent over the course of a whole year? Making up a flask of coffee at home in the morning will save you a huge amount of money that can instead stay in your account and be used for investment and long term income. Take a food pack-up with you a couple of times a week as much for the variety of taste and flavour as for the money savings.

What about the files, binders and unopened Financial Post that is stashed around your home and taking up useful shelf space or occupying the cupboard under the stairs? Get these all out and in one session go through them. If you have any papers that are more than a year old shred and dispose of them. A small shredder for your home will occupy far less space than the volume of unneeded statements, letters, documents and general papers that are taking up space in your life and adding to the stagnant energy we mention elsewhere in this book. If you run a business from home you will need to check with your Tax or Revenue office about the timescale for keeping all financial transaction records, and comply with these requirements. In many cases keeping the detail for the past twelve months and good annual summaries for the previous five to seven years is more than adequate for you and allows for a lot of discarding.

So many phone records, Bank statements, Insurance documents, Mortgage summaries and payment records can be accessed online and pulled down in Document or PDF format when needed. Review all your accounts and look at the options for switching to digital only records. This not only saves space but can also save you dozens of hours over the course of a year where you no longer have to open, sort, file and store paper that comes in to your physical mailbox.

Use Tools to Help Yourself.

Stay up to date with Financial Apps that allow you to track your spending or monitor your investment monies easily and all from your phone or laptop. Have you looked at installing a Water Meter to your home so you only get billed for your actual use? How about asking your Energy Company for a free Smart Meter to monitor your home usage of gas and electric? With these installed you can actively manage the way you use energy in your home, often adjusting your behaviour simply because you become aware of the cost of your usage. It can be tiring to deal with the potential mountain of financial paperwork that comes in to your home. Take a moment to consider that no matter how many sources the paperwork comes from you can choose what to do with each letter or email.

Stop being a Slave to Your Paperwork!

I maintain several properties that we rent out to individuals on a room by room basis. Each house requires a folder for utilities, tax records, rental income, finance costs, cleaning services, purchase of furniture, bedding, carpets and maintenance work. Each house has a subsection within a folder for tenants, all filed alphabetically by surname. One year after a tenant leaves I shred all records of correspondence with them and all their personal details. The housing paperwork is our largest block of paperwork for any ongoing theme and still it only fills a dozen large binders. I don't keep those at home, but instead maintain the paperwork in a small office cum storeroom in one of the buildings.

The new space for paperwork has come about by adding upright bookshelves to a small room and using these for keeping stuff neatly and off the floor. Before I got organised and started the letting go process, I had paperwork all over the place and wasted a few hours each week looking for documents. In the old days the paperwork, post and document files, tool kits, tins of paint, and new bedding sets messily took up a room that has now been let as a tidy and well furnished bedroom. The difference in getting organised for just this one example can easily be measured by the $100 a week rent I receive on that bedroom. The paperwork is organised and easy to reference while the income on that house has gone up by $5,200 a year from a space that was being poorly utilised previously. Nowadays when I visit the office space once each week I can collect and file all my post that same day.

Establish Paperwork Routines.

In your personal finances deal with each monthly summary statement as it comes in, whether by paper or email. Check the expenditure against your own receipts. An easy way to do this is to take any purchase receipts from your purse or wallet on a certain day each week and put them in a place where you do your finances. If you don't have any specific filing area at home, each week take the expense receipts for that week and place them in an envelope. When your bank statement comes in simply check off the purchase receipts against the larger monthly statement. Everything should match. If you are self-employed and doing your own tax returns save each weekly envelope and date it for easy reference later. When the full tax year is done you can provide the bank statements and the receipts to your book-keeper and you keep your costs down because you have taken the time to be organised for the previous year of spending.

The benefits of being more financially organised include greater peace of mind because you know where things are, more relaxation because you spend less time worrying and less wasted money because you are not repeat buying things that you thought you lost among the clutter. The less time you spend looking for things the more time you can allocate to building your wealth as distinct from simply monitoring what you have. Good decisions are not supported by chaos, disorganisation or by having to look for information.

As you sort, organise and structure your financial records you will naturally be drawn to look at their performance and the creation of more financial security and enhanced rewards from your activity. This is not only about organising your investment statements, but just as much relates to how you manage your online auction listings or manage the process of finding, booking and getting ready for attending the events you go to with your side hustle in crafting or small business.

Beware Wasted Purchases!

When we moved house recently we found seven dust pan and brush sets in our collection! Several had been bought to replace ones we thought we had lost or which we imagined I had bought and taken to work for the rental properties. No, they were in fact found in shopping bags that had never been emptied and become hidden among the masses of accumulated baggage from emptying the car or things left in the garage ready for being moved elsewhere. Six of these sets had been bought thinking that we needed something we already had.

If I have done that with something as simple as a $5 item, what might I have done in buying $500 beds or furniture items through lack of remembering what we had versus what we needed to buy. Each time you find yourself ending up with a duplicate of something you already have, be quick to learn the lesson that you are not as organised as you thought, and get the spare item back to the shop for the refund of the cash!

In becoming better organised with our finances we can get closer to our financial goals, precisely because we know what our money is doing and how it is performing. By getting clear on your financial paperwork, statements and information, you will naturally find yourself better able to make decisions about what to do with your assets so that they start to work for you, building your future wealth and financial freedom. The clearer you get with your finances now, the more certain it is that your money will work better for you.

SEVEN

Digital clutter

IN OUR CURRENT state of digital connection and constant online access there is always a temptation, a distraction away from the core values we once espoused and were driven by. How many hundreds of times have you sat at your laptop or device with the intention of taking 10 minutes to connect and catch up before getting on with the core task that you wanted to focus on and to achieve for the day, only to find yourself two hours later, adrift in the weird world of social media and without the energy or perhaps even the memory for that quickly forgotten priority? Apparently, we can check our mobile phone as much as 150 times in a day! Sound familiar?

Everyone wants your attention, from Facebook, to Instagram, to LinkedIn, Spotify, and Snapchat. You receive updates from coupon companies, cinema promotions, local events, requests for a Like from a business, an Invite from a friend who is starting a side hustle. Someone likes a Tweet you made, so you look at their profile and their feed for anything of interest. The technology behind the cell phone in your hand is far greater than a corporate super computer from twenty years ago. Each time you check a feed or a status update your brain gets a dopamine kick that serves your need for more points of data consumption. Friends of friends or even perhaps your own friends are leading lives of incredible ostentation, shopping, overseas travel and perfect family lives. Or so it seems when you click and watch, click and gawp, click and waste your time.

You have the ability to use online access thoughtfully and consciously, so why don't you? If you work eight or nine hours a day and come home to look at your screen while eating instead of connecting with family, if you lose hours every evening in wandering from one digital feed to another, then you can lose dozens of hours in a week. That same time, when used with deliberation and intent, can deliver to you additional free time for family, for love, for the accomplishment of your goals and for the investment of your energies into activities and hobbies that you love.

Spending time in these chosen blocks of time is what makes you who you are at your best, allows people to enjoy your company, and gives you that connection to the values you hold so important and which - if I were to ask you about them - you could reel off easily. What matters is not being able to talk about them, but having the ability, capacity and available time to spend your energies in such actions. A few years ago a poem by Gary Turk was going around, online of course, in a five minute film called "Look Up". It was a spoken word call to a cell phone generation. "Look Up" is a lesson taught to us through a love story, in a world where we continue to find ways to make it easier for us to connect with one another, but always results in us spending more time alone. Rather than engage constantly with your screen take time to consciously look at the world we inhabit, to have eye contact with people as you walk on a street and travel on a bus or a tube. To look up at the signs and art and window displays and at the great kindness and beauty around us. To connect with people rather than pass them by without even realising they were in the same space as you.

With acknowledgement to Gary, here are the first two verses of his poem.

Look Up

I have 422 friends, yet I am lonely.
I speak to all of them everyday, yet none of them really know me.
The problem I have sits in the spaces between,
looking into their eyes, or at a name on a screen.

I took a step back, and opened my eyes,
I looked around, and then realised
that this media we call social, is anything but
when we open our computers, and it's our doors we shut.
Gary Turk.

To guard your time you must, of necessity, manage your online time with forethought and consideration of what matters most. You need to take control of your time and to plan to maximise the time engaged in these points of enjoyment and satisfaction. What value two hours lost in watching random rubbish on viral feeds when you have told yourself that you will get a new language learned these next six months? How can you justify four hours lost one afternoon on a box set binge of eight episodes of a drama or comedy that steals the time away from your goal of setting up a lucrative side hustle that will repay your significant college loans, the same debts that keep you awake at night.

Device Addition?

Here are some practical steps can you take to reduce time lost forever to the state I refer as 'device addiction'. You can create some simple rules for yourself, or guidelines if you want to be less dramatic or at risk of your own control.

1. Switch your phone off for certain times during the day
2. Don't have it in your bedroom at night.
3. Have regular times when you are not accessible by phone.
4. When you are in one call do not put the first person on hold to take the second call.
5. Use voicemail as an aid to help you reduce stress, only pick up messages on a regular basis, perhaps twice a day or four times a day and not just because your phone beeps to tell you there is a message.
6. Have separate email accounts for different

roles of your life so you only check the one that is relevant at a given moment.

7. Check your personal email just once a day. It really can wait.
8. Check your work email at certain times throughout the day, perhaps twice in the morning and again twice in the afternoon.
9. Use a footnote in your outbound emails that suggests the timescale within which you will review and respond.
10. Set up an auto responder to incoming email that clearly states your availability or lack of availability to respond.

In the same way that it is rude to take one call when you are already in a call, how do you think colleagues, friends and family feel if you take calls when you are in the middle of a conversation with them? If a meeting is interrupted by a phone call that could have waited, you have not only caused a distraction and a loss of focus for yourself, but you have imposed that on everyone else by taking a call. It's not just about taking the call. If five people are in a meeting or gathering and they all have cell phones, beeping, vibrating or ringing, then all five will be distracted by looking at their devices. If you have a rule that phones are not to be used in the meeting, you will actually be more productive, will connect in a better way and get things done.

Real communication face to face is not served at all by people looking at their phones, however discreet or subtle they think they are about this. Next time you are out for a coffee or a meal with friends or are in a work meeting, switch your phone off and let other people see you are doing it, ask them to follow suit and explain that *"I want to be able to give this my full attention and can always collect a message when we are out of here."* The truth is that people might need help with understanding the significance of doing this themselves, but if you are not trying to share some of your values (including this desire to connect properly with someone), then maybe remind yourself how you want to do what works and live in alignment with your values.

We all use text or SMS to connect differently, but consider what your own style is. Do you send a message with all the content that is needed for the recipient, or do they then have to message or call you back to find out why you messaged them. An example of a wasted SMS message is one that says *"Hi Nick, please call me."* That means nothing to anyone. Is it urgent? Is there an emergency? Could the sender be bored? With a message like that I learn nothing.

I want a tenant to instead send me a message that says: *"Hi Nick, it's Paul at house ten. Nothing urgent. The washing machine drum has failed this morning. I just wanted you to know so that you can arrange an inspection and repair."*

Learn about their Communication Preference.

How you communicate digitally is one thing, but do you know how the other person uses technology? You might be a person who always has their phone within reach or at hand and with the volume on. But what if you are communicating with someone who always has the volume off and only looks at their phone four times a day? You will be frustrated without knowing why you are not getting a response. Become aware of the different communication styles of friends and colleagues and begin to adapt while also letting them know how you use your technology so they know how to reach you and when to anticipate a response.

A constant source of amusement for me are the people who call my cell phone, perhaps three or four times, but never send a text to say why they are ringing. Or a company will call me, not go through to voicemail, but not think to send me an email, especially if I have indicated email is my preferred communication when I signed up for their service or offering. I deliberately don't use voicemail because I would rather have a detailed text or an email than lose time on the phone when a written message would have done the same thing in less time. My friends know this so are no longer frustrated, but I do know that new callers can struggle to understand this until we meet up in person or are able to connect by telephone and I explain my reasons why!

Having a Digital Clear Out.

In looking at digital clutter I want to to take you to your tech equipment and look at the games, software and apps which eat at your available time. How many games have you got on your cell phone that you never play? Remove the apps completely and free up storage. What about financial apps that you used a few times before forgetting or ignoring months ago? Delete them right now.

How about photos that use up huge amounts of data on your PC, laptop or cell phone? In a recent deletion process I realised I had 2,400 pictures on my macbook and synchronised in Google photos which I no longer needed. These spanned several years and gave me many great memories. But I also had pictures in huge volume of several people I was no longer in contact with, and hundreds of pictures I had taken of building inspections and room assessments.

Remember that outside of my writing life I am a residential landlord with some shared houses. Every time a tenant leaves I take perhaps twenty images of the room, and when that same room has been cleaned, tidied, prepped and made ready for a new tenant I go through the same process so that the new resident has a record of what the room was like when they took it on. For some reason, I found I had photo sets taken years before and which were still occupying storage on my devices long after a tenancy had ended and a room had been relet to someone new. I went through every image and deleted hundreds. When you do this you can load hundreds of images onto a USB device, or a portable or remote hard drive. You can upload to a cloud account so your device runs faster and more smoothly. You can install favourite images onto a digital photo frame so that you actually get to see the images you love and which mean something to you.

Practical Steps for a Digital Declutter.

Here are some ideas and suggestions for making the best use of your physical space where you work with digital equipment, as well as the invisible space that your data occupies.

Organising your folders.

Be cautious of any folder still called New Folder and check the contents before you rename it. If you can't find what you want it may be hiding in a folder that is incorrectly labelled. Have sub folders within a Group folder. For example, for writing and preparing this book I have a Group folder called Declutter on my MacBook. Within this are files called Declutter Diary, Declutter Sales, Declutter Manuscript, Declutter Mood Boards. Each time you name a folder it will then save alphabetically, so make sure you know your Group folders.

Have a Group folder for each role that you have in your life. For example, mine include : Family, Household, Author, Investor, and Landlord. Inside each of these you can have multiple separate folders i.e. Family might contain Dad, Partner, Budget, Diary, Finance, Holidays, School.

Old Documents.

Open each folder and look at the documents. Do you need to keep each one? How many are no longer necessary? What information is worth keeping? Delete where you can and free up storage space, but also the mental distractions from continually sorting. If in doubt create an Archive folder and move some documents in.

Your Email Inbox.

Just as you go through your physically delivered post each day, apply the same principle to your inbox. Rather than go past the emails that are not important when you first elect what to read, start instead to delete what you know you will not open. Keep your Inbox to the minimum. Once read it should be moved out of the Inbox and to a Subject Folder that is indexed by category and easy to find. Have relevant Sub Themes to a Folder. Have specific times in a day when you will look at email.

Photos.

Keep the ones that you love, that really mean something and delete all the others. If some pictures might be good for someone else, check if they want them and email them across, cleaning them from your storage afterwards.

Old Apps and Software.

Whether on your phone or desktop make sure to remove the programmes you don't use, don't want or which you cannot remember installing. You can delete a link but must also check to uninstall the actual software you don't want. This will continue to release space on your hard drive.

Icons.

On your home screen or desktop the images that sit there take up screen space and distract you from a clean environment. Tidy them up and remove them where you can.

Films and Music.

These are huge data users and so much is now available on listening platforms either free when in a wifi zone or by subscription if you think it work spending the money to carry the music with you wherever you go. You can also use YouTube and various platforms for revisiting the tracks and films you want.

USB sticks.

Check your desk drawers and bag pockets for these. These are powerful and small, often carrying so much more data than you can remember by name. They are easy to lose, precisely because of their size. Open each one you have and check the files and documents stored. Do you need them and if you do, have you already got them on your main laptop or desktop machine? Could the same information or files be stored in the cloud? Often we carry duplicate docs on a USB that are simply copies taken from an email attachment. If so then we can delete either the email or delete the file on the memory stick. Imagine your panic if you were to lose a USB with hundreds of docs when you neglected to get round to editing and cleaning content from it. Keep you empty USBs in a place where you might also keep fresh stationery and pens in your desk.

Email Newsletters.

Remove yourself from all the lists where you are no longer interested or where the content is no longer relevant for you. Find the unsubscribe link. Remove all unwanted back issues from your inbox.

Email accounts.

There are a few schools of thought on this one. The minimalist will go for a maximum of two accounts as being enough, one for work and the other for personal or social. I am happy with one for my private life and several others for each my different working or business roles. Find what you consider is simple and obvious to your circumstances.

Contacts Information.

Make a coffee and sit down to review your Contacts file. Go through it and delete the names you no longer need, are not meeting any more or where you consider there is no longer a value. If you are an inveterate networker and think that everyone might at some point be helpful, useful or potentially serve as a good introducer for you, then you will of course struggle with this exercise. Be brave and delete. Or contact them and save or delete based on their response to your offer.

Password Info.

Some swear by a single password for everything. Others like to find a common theme and work with a slight adjustment to their core password structure but with a tag or reference that might be linked to the name of the website they login to or visit. If you have accounts where you cannot remember the log in detail, face the fact that you perhaps don't make much use of the site and delete the entire account or create a generic password you can remember through a memory jog word or question.

Physical Technology Devices.

The longer you have been online the more old pieces of kit will be filling your desk drawers and cupboard space. Pull it all out and recognise that most of it has been surpassed, made simpler, made cheaper or made to work faster than the old items you can throw away. Old cell phones, camera equipment, cables, data storage devices. Are some of them worth selling on an auction site?

Internet Browser.

If you are getting easily distracted by news headlines or sports stories when you log on, then choose a simpler version of the browser. Remove yourself from all the tabbed interests available.

Downloads.

You may have hundreds of these cluttering your data space. Click on Downloads, look at what you have. For the items that are worth keeping move them to a relevant folder to find them again. Bin everything else.

Manuals and Instruction CDs.

Almost all digital devices now have instruction guidance that can be found online as a PDF or on a manufacturers download pages. Throw the paper manuals, binders and CDs that are taking up a shelf in your study. Recycle what you can and bin the rest.

Behavioural Steps for avoiding Lost Digital Time.

It's one thing to take practical actions against continuing to store data that no longer serves your aims, it's quite a different matter to behave in ways that waste your time or pull you away from those things you consider important.

Cut your Social Media Addiction.

It's time for you to impose a set limit on the amount of time you spend spend on social media, regardless of which platforms you are a regular or even heavy user of. Rather than go cold-turkey overnight, you are better to fix an amount of time and start with this. How many hours a day are you connected to your social platforms? Cut an hour from that tomorrow and work forward from there. Aim towards a morning catch up and an evening catch up, perhaps twenty minutes on each. You do not need any more than that. How different might your life be if you were to take the time 'spent' on Social Media and move it to activities that increase your personal health, well being and actual happiness?

FACEBOOK.

These 623 Friends are not your friends. When you need to cry over a bereavement they will not all be there. When you are lonely and scared about something talk to a real friend, grab a coffee with a real person and just 'talk'. If you are nervous about what people think, before you cull the numbers, start by clicking the 'Unfriend' button. They can still follow your activity, but you no longer get the updates about lives you are not really interested in. Could you consider the fact that a post once or twice a week is more genuine than four posts a day. Are there twenty people you want to spend time with this year? Pick up the phone and call them. If you really do care about a video showing a cat jumping away from a cucumber, or a beautiful family that you have never met showing off with the graduating daughter, or the poolside party life, ask yourself why these things merit your attention in a life that only has a set number of hours and minutes. Me, a cynic? No. I use Facebook and Instagram sparingly as potentially helpful networking tools, but only for a daily average of 15 minutes twice a day.

Understand this. Social Media is not the same as a 'social life'.

GAMES.

Addictive, fun and time suckers. Scrabble, Game of Thrones, Medal of Honour, Chess, Candy Crush, etc. Do you have to play a game? What is it and why do you play it? Rather than living in escapism, can you let it go and instead use your time to work on your goals for the real world?

Ok, that's my rant over and I hope you will please forgive me. I enjoy Pinterest to get inspiration for home decor, Instagram for selling vintage books and Facebook mainly for the messenger facility when I am at a desk and actually have wifi switched on. But I like to limit my non-email online time to no more than 30 minutes each day. There is so much more to do.

Remember that this is a book about decluttering, about letting go of the physical things that get in the way of the life you want to lead. The added digital distraction posed by social media is a massive potential drain of your time and focus away from what matters for you in leading a value driven life. If you want to see radical change in your daily life, just start to switch off your wifi access for several hours each day and watch how much quality time you find. Notice the effects of this on your sense of self and what is important to you in your own life. You are NOT your social media accounts!

EIGHT

Help me please, I'm a hoarder!

YOU WILL REMEMBER that I told you we moved house in order to live with less and intentionally reduce our costs. The first section of this chapter is largely taken from my own journal and notes from the weeks around that move.

Journal Entry

First week of our move.

Yesterday I was at work in my office. The word office for this room might seem somewhat grand because it also doubles as a store room for furniture that I have not dared throw away, just in case it might be useful one day when a tenant needs it. So in addition to my much loved roll-top pine bureau with plentiful drawers and cubbyholes, you will see two enormous vintage 1940's wardrobes that I am hanging on to just in case I decide one day to add them into some of the upstairs bedrooms in this building. I have two double mattresses, a nicely upholstered Edwardian straight backed hall seat for two, a solid wood filing cabinet and, in the alcoves to either side of the fireplace, a pair of tall glass fronted book cabinets. The ample floor space in this room is normally free of clutter, but this week I have made numerous car trips into work with the boxes that were filling my garage at home. I have been doing this before we move house - right in the middle of writing a book about decluttering and letting go - as apart of a deliberate decision to live with less and in a space that is better suited to the life we want to live.

I have eighty boxes to work through and the emotional pain of doing this is significantly more than I was expecting. These are the boxes that I have dragged around with me between homes for a number of years and which I have to open now that we are settling somewhere. I understand that this is not normal, that someone my age would by now have perhaps cracked the clutter code and found a way to let go of so much. I have never found this easy, and have always attached emotions, possibility or potential re-use to things that I have had in my life.

Box One. *I opened the first box and realised that not one of several thousand sheets of papers in any of the ring-bound folders in the box were to keep. Most of them had a keep-until date that had passed at least two years before. I had kept them as the Revenue service always ask you to keep the paperwork for a business for seven years after the year represented by those same records. I hadn't thrown them away because I hadn't dared approach the task of sorting, sifting and saying goodbye to them. The box of files weighed fully 20 pounds. I separated the paper from the files and recycled it all. So far, so good. I can do this.*

Box Two. *Two dozen used A4 pads of lined writing paper, 65 usable pens, a hole punch, a vintage wood and brass manual coffee grinder in good order that I had been given by friends in Belgium when I was perhaps eighteen. That was some decades* *ago. I had wondered where it was! The pads of notepaper went onto a stationery shelf, and the pens went into a plastic bag for donating to my local library. They are always running out of pens and I love to work there on new manuscripts, so this feels like a good outcome.*

Box Three. *Some small card boxes of new one inch screws. A thoughtful 'remember me' gift from a former girlfriend which had been sent to me unannounced at my new address the Christmas after we broke up. It was a finely sculpted wooden head on a stand, designed to take a pair of reading glasses. Cute, but completely forgotten. It was still in the padded bag it had arrived in and a handwritten note "Good luck in your new life x." I felt sad, pleased to be away from that, and disappointed in myself that I had carried the object and the associated negative karma of it around in my life for the subsequent seven years. Next to this another envelope containing an almost new looking set of souvenir postcards from a visit to Uzbekistan that I had made 22 years before! This was a total surprise. I could not remember buying them or perhaps having been given them by my hosts for that trip. A box of marbles from my own childhood. A wooden chest containing an old pub game and which I remembered buying in a beautiful antique shop on a sunny day in Monmouth four years ago. I bagged up the love gift, the marbles and the pub game and placed them in a pile for the charity shop, our goodwill store.*

Going through just these three boxes took me almost an hour. I calculate that more than two thirds of the stuff within the boxes, by volume, was binned. The pens can be used by the library staff and the rest goes to have a new life via the charity shop. When I saw the note with the wooden gift I didn't cry, but I was upset and sad. Sad that something once so good and joyful did not last. Upset that I had hung onto an item knowing I would never use it, believing since opening it that I would have returned it to her, yet consciously allowing it to take up physical space, less aware of the subtle emotional toll."

Just goes to prove that I keep my own journals!

Justifying my own Hoarding Behavior.

I am not going to list the contents of every box that I went through as a part of that decision we made to move house. I know it will take me a while to go through the lot of them one by one, binning, recycling and perhaps giving away or donating the contents once I have revisited them. Many of the boxes contain just books and these will be simpler to sort. I have decided to let go of all the popular fiction books as these have little financial value and are easy items for charity shops to resell and gain a bit of money from. I will keep the non-fiction books, perhaps a thousand titles and list these online for their vintage or collectable value. One poetry I book I have held for years has a likely value of $800 - $1,000 if I am not too greedy for the highest price and several hundred have a value to collectors of more than $40 per book. The rest will go for between $5 and perhaps $15 per title. Of course, such items only have a financial value at the point that a buyer hands over or transfers the funds to become the new owner. Until then each book is still clutter.

Consider this fact as you think about your own clutter that can potentially be donated. If you take it to the thrift store just a couple of shopping bags at a time, you are giving up minutes or part hours of your time in doing this. Choose the closest store and let it go quickly. Here's the thing. Once you have let it go, it doesn't matter at all what you might have been able to sell it for. It's gone now. "Over and done with!", just like the great song by The Proclaimers. Move on now.

It's official! I can now confess to having Hoarding Disorder.

I knew I was a 'Collector', and always preferred that title more. It started out as a school boy given a stamp album and collecting the bags of franked stamps, looking through the magnifying glass for rare marks, unusual countries, changed country names. Then it moved into other costly hobbies, collecting medals, uniforms. After university and working for a living I started to collect houses, not just the one but dozens of them, buying them and renting them out. Nowadays I know that the brain of someone like me works in a way that has been diagnosed as an actual medical condition, categorised and understood by psychologists.

People who are hoarders go overboard in the saving of items that other people will regard as worthless. The hoarder apparently struggles in parting with possessions, and this leads to clutter that gets in the way of effectively using their homes or work spaces. Yes, that's been me. I think I can say that I certainly tick that box! My journal entries from the time of that move showed me for sure that I was struggling with the disorder.

Do you have Hoarding Disorder?

Hoarding and collecting are distinct activities. The collector will search out specific items, working to a list or a recommendation of what will be popular or have greater value in the future. They are likely to display their items in a presentable and ordered manner. When an item is placed within an established collection, it is allocated a special almost magical status. By combining it with other connected or somehow similar pieces, the one acquires more value than it was deemed to have when on its own. Popular acceptance suggests that a collection has a value, yet it is only seen this way by other collectors of that niche area.

The truth is that organised collections give to their owners a sense of importance, and are a socially acceptable form of possessiveness. There is social prestige and enhanced status in the mind of the collector of high value items that are brought together under one roof, endorsing their social standing within their community or peer group. Someone who collects watercolour pictures, ceramics from a specific historic timeframe, or vintage cars is seen to be an eccentric, albeit perhaps an affluent one.

The hoarder is not so discriminate and simply gathers random things which they consider they might want in the future. For some, they find safety in the volume of their possessions. Looking at some statistics from the American Psychiatric Association and their Diagnostic and Statistical Manual of Mental Disorders we learn that hoarding disorder affects some 2 to 6% of the adult population and often leads to substantial distress and problems functioning in daily life. Now I am getting worried about my behaviour! In a UCLA scale of Hoarding Severity (who even knew there was such a thing!) males are more likely to succumb to this behaviour than females and it is three times more predominant in older males than in those aged 34 to 44 years old.

More on the Science of Hoarding.

We know that when faced with a drawer full of junk it can be very difficult to throw away things we have no regular use for. A study at Yale School of Medicine has been able to track the brain function that we go through when faced with such decisions as keep or throw, save or toss. The school invited a mixed group of hoarders and non-hoarders to meet with them for research and asked the group to sort through items such as old newspapers and junk mail. The test was structured to include items that belonged to the researcher and other items belonging to the participant. Those taking part had to decide on what to keep and what to discard and while they were doing this the research team tracked the brain activity of those sifting through the items.

When faced with how to deal with their own stuff that had been included in the observed test, the hoarders had increased activity in two areas of the brain, the Anterior Cingulate Cortex (ACC) and the Insula. The greater the struggle that the hoarder felt about whether to throw something out, the more this pattern of brain activation was recorded. The activation of the trigger between the ACC and Insula sections of our brain is creating a message that there is 'something wrong' and we need to defend ourselves against the doubt or uncertainty. Keep the item and the unease reduces. These two areas of the brain are moved into play when a smoker wants to give up tobacco or an addict approaches the decision to quit the drug they use. Keep the cigarette and the fear of loss weakens. The greater the activation of the two parts of the brain, the more we feel discomfort, unease and anxiety and so we reach again for the cigarette.

Compulsive shoppers also recognise the same brain activity when faced with a high price on an item. They can put lesser priced items in their trolley all day long if this feeling makes them restful and happy while they accumulate, but when faced with a high priced item, the brain message allows them to push the item away and move to something where the brain has no threat-response activation. This process can be an explanation of why there is a strong self-sustaining element involved in the behaviour of the hoarder. When we find and decide to hold onto an item, we feel calmer and all is good with our world.

Do you struggle to throw out books, or clothes or beer bottles from different breweries? If you like reading, dressing yourself a certain way or have a nostalgia for drinking games from college days, then let's see what the link might be. Other research into hoarder behaviour has shown activation of another area of the brain, the ventromedial PreFrontal Cortex (or vmPFC).

The more this is activated the greater the feeling we have of wanting something. It is often the case that the item we are attracted to reinforces our sense of "Me" or of "This is who I am".

If you have a tendency to hoard and to accumulate it might be that you are seeing those books sitting on shelves or stacked on your stairs as a reflection of who you think you are, or those wardrobes jammed with clothes as who you are when walking out in the world, or of those old beer bottles with different labels as reflecting back to you how much fun you had with your drinking games. Recognising how the vmPFC element of your brain is activated by the books or bottles, which others see just as junk or mess, can help you understand that you no longer need all this to be who you are.

You may have Hoarding Disorder if :

You struggle to let go go items because you think they should be saved and where you get distressed over the idea of letting them go.

The volume of things piled high, stacked, and placed within your home space makes it difficult for you to move about freely.

You buy things or always accept free things that you don't need and for which you don't have space anyway.

You have difficulty discarding, donating, recycling or otherwise gifting things that other people would be unlikely to keep in their house after use.

This can lead to a lot of belongings stashed at home and cluttering up walk ways through the home, presenting an obstacle course that is also likely to become a fire hazard. It is likely to lead to strain and conflict within the family, but also can lead to isolation and loneliness due to the fact that others - potential partners - will not understand the problem when they see it and want to avoid living with it, or because the hoarder knows that the behaviour is potentially a block to social activity and the embarrassment of inviting people home to discover the accumulation of possessions.

As well as the behavioural difficulties in discarding, of constantly saving items, packaging and clutter, many compulsive hoarders have the difficulties which come from disorganisation, indecision and perfectionism bordering on OCD. Such traits can make their private lives difficult as well as impacting on their social lives where they rarely allow people into their home space for fear of ridicule, shame or guilt at their inability to manage the possessions they have gathered together in the one space.

Why do we Hoard?

The simple act of owning something can create in our brain the perception of value. There are thousands of identical books to the comic book you have or that edition of a monthly magazine, but your mind will assign value to it precisely because it your copy of that book or magazine. The sense of owning something and attributing it a value, is referred to as the Endowment Effect. We give that value to something because it is ours.

House builders want to get you in the show house because it has been made to look real, it has been decorated and filled with gorgeous furniture. This is done so that the endowment effect will work in your brain and emotionally push you forward to where you imagine yourself owning it. The same is true of a car dealership where the sales person wants you to sit in the vehicle and drive it. This way you get a physical as well as deeply emotional sense of what it would be like to own the object.

You can break down or reduce the power of the endowment effect by asking a simple question :

"How much effort would I put in to get hold of this, if I didn't own it already?"

The hoarder holds on to things that are easy to acquire rather than items of value which require money to be spent or effort to be invested. Associated with this ease of acquisition you will see the link between hoarding and gifts that are given to us.

Often we will hang on to a wedding present, even if we don't particularly like it, because it came to us easily and there was no effort involved. Part of this equation is the ease with which a hoarder accumulates things, but the other issue is that of the guilt we feel we would experience if we were to throw away or donate the item. All of this is in your head by the way. None of it is real. You own a set of crockery that came as a gift. Smash it up. Throw it away. Donate it to the goodwill shop. There is no guilt attached to the plates. It is only your thinking that is applying this. Other people just see a set of plates.

Hoarding and Your Past.

There will be some elements of your past that hold one or two keys to your current 'grown-up' world of hanging onto things or even to obsessive hoarding. Taking time to look at these and to journal about what you observe and learn can be very helpful. I gather books around me like they will never be printed again. Pens fill my house. Stationery is something I value as a jeweller might adore diamonds. If I take these three points of clutter I can see where the root of my addiction begins. It starts with childhood.

As the first of seven children there was always a younger sibling who would see something I had and want it for themselves. It was often a pen or pencil that I used for schoolwork which would disappear to be used for scribbling or colouring in a book. A book I had been given when pre-school and which I remembered even then having read to me by my Mum or Dad, would be pulled by a brother or sister and the pages would be ripped or smudged or be covered in their food.

At some point I must have had the thought that:

"I need more pens because they are always being taken" or

"I need to put my books out of reach so that my sisters can't get hold of them".

And so my gathering of books and stationery began. It just never stopped!

When I am in a bookstore I go weak at the knees with the desire to buy at least one book and take it home. Often for the reading of the story that I am attracted to from the cover blurb, but always more for the sense of ownership, of being able to say *"these books are mine"*. I have exactly the same sensations when I am in the stationery department of a store, or even better, if I am in a shop that only sells pens. Biros, fountain pens, brushed metal pens, gel pens, propelling pencils, erasers, pencil sharpeners. Surrounded by these I am in heaven.

Case in Point re my own Stationery Hoarding.

Consider this ridiculous piece of information relevant to this chapter. I am writing in the local library this morning and my pencil case is next to my laptop. Given what I have just been writing about I have emptied the case onto the table and find I have eighteen pens with me. Not a couple but eighteen. For evidence of my OCD tendencies (at least I can embrace it) here are the details:

4 fountain pens, blue ink.

5 gel pens, black ink.

5 biros, black ink.

4 felt pens, red, green, brown and blue ink.

Why do I have so many pens around me? I am writing on a laptop at this stage of the book before I print and then do an edit by hand and with a pen. I use a paper diary and can use that with just three pens of different colours. Why don't I have just three pens with me today when I am primarily putting my thoughts down on a laptop? I have so many pens precisely because their presence gives me a sense of who I am with the *"I am a writer"* part of my identity, but also because I made the decision as a teenager that I would always make sure I had enough of what I wanted and which other people could not take away from me. Even now I am protecting myself from fear of loss. That's an interesting observation for me to add to the journal later! These things will just continue to surprise you as you start and then add to your own journal as you go through this process of Letting Go. We learn from the very same insights we can help ourselves to reach.

Learning to Surf the Urge!

Games we can play with our mind in order to reduce the impact of accumulated junk in our lives can include the process of moving towards the item we think we want, but with the consideration that we are just in a game. We can pick up the item and hold it. How does it make us feel? How does it then feel when you place it back on the counter or put it back on the shelf in the bookstore. When I am in a large city centre I enjoy browsing in the bookstores and sometimes I commit to going in and just looking, to knowing that I will wander around the store and leave without purchasing a book. Interestingly, in a small indie bookshop, and especially in the shops that sell second hand or vintage books, I don't feel the same urge.

In a big bookstore of new books I will find a few books of interest and take them over to a comfy chair. I will spend twenty minutes looking at the books and their content, at the author bio and the jacket blurb. I will satisfy the urge inside my brain that loves the smell of freshly printed clean pages and a cover that has no blemishes or rips. Then I will leave the store and congratulate myself on having enjoyed myself without spending money.

Walk Away from Hoarding.

I have been to the edge of the thrill, but faced the addiction and walked away from it. I have surfed the urge. I have not succumbed to the temptation to own the item. Do this for yourself and find the correlation between getting the mental high from taking yourself to those places where you are normally driven by your brain to buy things to satisfy what your brain suggests you need, but then walking away.

Never an easy thing to do, we need to find ways to let go of the clutter of course, and that is what the whole book is looking at and dealing with. Specifically related to hoarding here are some questions which might be useful for you to work through :

"If I had to buy this object with my own money, would I do so again?"

"Knowing what space this collection of unworn clothes take up in my house, could I bag them up for either the waste bin or for donation to a charity shop?"

"Can I invite a good friend to help me deal with removing items from my house, for just one hour this week, and book with them to do the same again next week?"

"If I can I create just two rooms without clutter in my house, which rooms will I choose to work on first?"

"What can I learn about my hoarding behaviour by exploring the past that has shaped me and my approach to possessions?"

Admitting the existence of the problem is a huge aspect of freeing yourself up emotionally to deal with the clutter that is swamping your house. Opening up to friends and family to speak with them about how you feel over the issue of your junk swamping your living environment is a strong way forward. You are dealing with a state of mind that is recognised as an aspect of mental health.

Good luck with seeking help, and also for finding practical support with the clearing of things that are covering up surfaces and filling the cupboards and storage areas of your home. You can do something about this where it is causing you to feel overwhelmed and lost. Don't be slow in coming forward and seeking support and guidance. When you take action, by dealing with just one shelf or one drawer at a time, you will make progress. Over time this repeated positive action will combine to give you increasingly good outcomes for you and the space you can enjoy living in.

NINE

The downsize life

ADVERTS TELL us to buy new, to acquire more, to 'go large' and so often we fall for the message that is pushed upon us. We are encouraged to lease a bigger car with greater luxury. We should own a house with more space, clear separation from the neighbouring property and a kitchen that is more like a chef's showroom than a place for enjoyable family dining. Of course, we are told that we need an extensive wardrobe that provides clothes for every season, but also for every month of the year, together with the absolute best of bags, watches and additional accessories. Each of these items comes with a well known and heavily branded label which we are expected to discreetly mention or simply show off to our friends.

Considering the Trade Off between Time and Opportunity.

In the coffee shop at my local library I recently had an unpleasant experience when I was writing. I heard a voice from my past and looked up to see a man who had once worked for a company I had bought buildings from. Ten bedrooms, fifty apartments, one hundred dwellings at a time and more. The process had been exciting, intoxicating at times but had ended badly and caused me several years of struggle after the collapse. The man I could see queuing for a coffee had been a part of that collapse, with behaviours that were criminal yet never prosecuted. Here he was again, as flamboyant as ever, with the gift of the smart patter and a touch of abundance. For a moment I wondered whether to creep out of the cafe without being seen, but thought better of it and walked over to introduce myself. He knew me instantly and recalled my name with ease. We chatted amiably for a few minutes before parting, but the awkwardness had passed by my making contact. I had seen a demon and faced it head on and felt better for it.

Sitting in the library again I mulled over the changes in my life since the heady days of property investment and resale and of the lifestyle we had enjoyed as a family then. It had indeed been one of good times for several years followed by a sudden ending and rapid financial collapse. In the years of ascendancy we could buy what we wanted, live where we chose and enjoy the comforts of good access to money. However, there were several years when I was away from home and staying in hotels on business for several nights a week. There were family dinners, celebrations and birthdays that I missed through not making myself available, and instead being addicted to the work and the chase of potential profit.

One incident in particular summaries how off-track I was at the time. I remember attending the funeral of my grandma, arriving by chauffeur driven car in a normal journey where I had been in the back seat and on my phone for every minute of the journey until arriving at the crematorium. I said a hello to my parents and siblings, present with them but detached from the goings on and the emotional sadness of the event that day, which was a celebration of the life of my Dad's own Mum, my grandmother. As soon as the service was over I was away again with my driver and with my phone glued to my head as we travelled on to another meeting. I didn't stay for the wake, for the customary chat over sandwiches and drinks and the opportunity to share stories of our Grandma. I let my siblings down with my actions, of course, but I massively let my Dad down even though he never said a word against me about it.

Seeing this man from my overly frantic and busy past, I had the opportunity to reflect on the change that has happened and where I had been lead through the circumstances that I endured. Fifteen years on and I am in a place where I am much happier, completely satisfied with my circumstances, living the indie lifestyle that my partner and I have created together. We chose to downsize recently and go through the declutter journey. We made a decision to look at what we need to be happy and solvent and at peace with our life. We took the steps necessary to make the income streams that have allowed us to pay off our debt and have around us those things which either bring joy or support our conscious move into what we refer to together as the Downsize Life.

What might you do to Improve Your Life?

This opportunity is real for you, for us all. It takes thought, effort and some determination to step away from those things which might well allow you to pay your bills, but perhaps come with an element of stress and worry. I am speaking here about the politics of a work organisation and the shenanigans that can take place there. But pettiness and upset are a part of life in any place where you have a lot of interaction with people, so don't think it's just about where you work! Let's get real about all of this.

First, give thought to all aspects of your life as they are now. Consider your existing accommodation, money and financial resources, lifestyle and health, your support network, and your future plans and goals. In identifying these different elements take the time to note how you feel emotionally about each one.

Do you love where you live? Not just the building or type of accommodation, but the surrounding environment and geography, landscape and neighbourhood. Are you happy with the physical space you occupy, with the structure and design of your home?

Retirement Years.

Re your money, are you earning what you need to live without worry or fear of debt? Is there a side hustle you can start to cover any shortfall for your cost of living or to begin the process of clearing your debts to other people or to credit organisations? What money have you set aside in a savings pot, both cash money for emergencies or unexpected bills, mid term money to give you a breathing space for three months or more in the event of illness, and real long term money that would allow you the freedom of stepping down from one job to take another where you will be happier and more fulfilled. What about the long game and being financially ready for retirement, fully prepared for the years of no job income?

Health and Well-Being.

Lifestyle and health matters are broad in theme and topic. Here I am asking you to look at the way you live and your physical wellbeing and fitness. So many external factors affect this, but you choose what you eat and the exercise you need and take daily. Food choices and the quality of this is important. Perhaps this ties in with the neighbourhood and local shops or access to the countryside, parks and gyms. Interaction with community groups and activities can be hugely valuable for your positive mental health and well-being.

Like Minded Friends and Support Networks.

Who you have around you as a support is critical. Friendships and networks of like minded people allow you to be your best you. They encourage you to follow your favourite activities and plans. They want you to win at the things which are important and special to you. Contact with friends in a real way, and not just online via social media, is good for your emotions and your mental health. Some of these people might be your neighbours. Others may be in your immediate family circle.

I enjoy contact with friends in a weekly writing group that I attend and who I love chatting with over a coffee. Each year I meet up with some volunteers and we clean, paint and decorate a youth hostel or community venue in preparation for the next season of heavy use by cyclists, climbers and young people on expedition groups.

Other friends are those I see each month in a social enterprise where they provide a pay-as-you-feel cafe above a food distribution warehouse that provides meal ingredients to community cooking groups.

Look at the people who are important to you and whose company you enjoy. If you want to expand your social life, you only have to search local noticeboards, both physically in local coffee shops and community venues, and of course in online forums and postings.

TEN

Enough is all you need

ENJOYING your Downsize Life is all about getting to the place where you are self-sufficient. I don't mean that you need to be living off the land, growing your own vegetables and distilling rain water for your shower and teaching your kids at home rather than using a state school system. What I am keen on is the idea that you can live in a house that meets all your needs for space and utility, that your work or paid employment is fulfilling, and that you have satisfaction and happiness in the physical environment you occupy.

Having enough to satisfy and meet these needs truly is all that you require. Having enough means you having sufficient resources. You can be a creative indie providing skills and services or products to your various clients. You could be a portfolio worker holding two or three separate roles which, when taken together, provide the finance that is enough to cover your bills for accommodation and food, for clothing, leisure time and future savings plans.

You may work in a secure job that you love or one in which you are uncomfortable and looking for a new role that provides greater fulfilment to your own values and sense of what you consider important and nurturing.

Possibly you are out of work and between jobs or in long term unemployment with little expectation of finding work again. In any one of these situations you are able to give thought and attention to how you live right now and whether there are aspects of it that you seek to adjust or adapt.

Enough is about being self-sufficient in whatever way works for you and your household. It is about being happy with how your life looks and works. Accepting the *Enough Is All You Need* mindset requires you to separate from what the adverts and the celebrity gossip columns suggest are important and to be admired, and to instead just consider what you want. Having enough for your needs is all you need. Ever.

In a modern, developed economy you are doing well if you have a financial surplus being saved each month. Apparently, more than 70% of working households would struggle to deal with something as simple as finding $750 - $1,000 for a surprise domestic bill, like the failure of the central heating boiler. If you can pay your bills and still have enough set aside for the inevitable surprise bill or incident where an extra $500 or $2,000 is needed, then you are in a good place. If you can do this and still have an enjoyable holiday a couple of times each year, you are way ahead of many people.

To get into an even more positive position, think

about taking away completely or significantly reducing any of the workplace stress or political troubles that come with employment in a larger work place where there is always someone above you, telling you what to do and by when, or giving you tasks to do which seem ever more difficult to achieve. To remove yourself from that needs an extra financial move requiring a radical reassessment of your own cost of living and survival each month. Where you can make significant downward adjustments to your regular outgoings, you are creating more flexibility in what work you choose to do to earn money and then to secure it.

This lifestyle requires you to listen to your heart and hear what your feelings are telling you. Where you feel anguish, worry, upset or simple unease, there is a message for you and an idea to explore. If you open your post and constantly see bills that are just beyond your ability to settle in full, this is a wake-up call to think about your monthly cost of living and start to look at cutting those costs so that you can live within your means to pay those same bills next month. If you have possessions you never use and where you have low emotional attachment to them, then they should be up for sale and gone.

If you have a three bedroom house and have no need for regularly hosting visitors can you be better off in a home with just one less bedroom, but which still accommodates your needs for personal space and storage? Would such a move either save you money in significantly reduced rent or allow you some greater flexibility over your choice of work? If you own your home and sold it to move into a different space that you buy for less, can the surplus you create by moving house then be used to boost your savings and reduce any debts for good? If you work in a place where conflict between employees is difficult, the quality of management is low, or where the rate of pay is poor, you can use these factors as motivation to find employment that better suits you.

Think about the areas of your life where you feel unhappy, stressed, worried or dissatisfied and consider how you could make things different. The easiest way to determine if there is a need for change, is to ask yourself: *"How am I coping?"* Listen to your mind and hear the honest answers that come out of this.

What does Your Space Do for You?

We recently went through the change from a big three bedroom house with a massive ground floor room that was lounge and dining area, and which also had a long front garden and small rear garden. We made little use of the large front space because it was open to view from the road, so we found ourselves always more naturally using the smaller rear garden. The place we moved to still has two gardens, but the proportions of them are reversed. The majority of the garden is at the back and so we are more relaxed in this new outside space.

The previous detached house was one we rented in a lovely and well thought of area of the local town. Just five minutes walk from our front gate we had a large public park and mature woodland. All great for us and walks with our Labrador! We had the main bedroom at the front of the house and which overlooked the garden and the busy road. At the back of the house, the guest bedroom and 'spare' room had the better garden views. Our so called 'spare' room had a double bed in it that was rarely used, and which had become our dumping ground for excess clothes, office papers, spare bedding and piles of books. Floorspace was reduced by a desk I used when working from home, a dressing table and a makeup table. Fitted wardrobes housed all our hung clothes and we also had a vertical clothes rack in there for drying. It was a real mess and felt like a no-go area every time I went in. The monthly cost to us for living here was £1,150 a month and this seemed like reasonable value at the time.

In our new home we still have three bedrooms in a semi-detached house (one that shares a wall with the neighbouring property) that we own and which is in a much less fashionable area, but still with a large public park within a few minutes walk. We have made our own bedroom into a beautiful space. The second room is a temporary home study with one complete wall of treasured books and storage for stationery. My property work files no longer come home with me. We each have a desk in this room with a printer between the his and hers desks. From this room we can run our side hustle together and I alternate my writing time between this calm private space and the fun and often crazy times writing at an open table in the local library. These rooms overlook the rear garden which is peaceful and attractive. The third room is a dedicated dressing room with a comfy single bed for when we have a guest stay with us. The whole arrangement is one where the space is better used, and the function of each room has become clearer.

Now we are happier in our space and have noticed our home environment is calmer. The way we use the house is more clearly defined and we have more energy for the hobbies and pastimes we love. I have purchased a large wooden shed to be constructed at the bottom of the garden as a creative writing space separate from the house and we then get to convert the other spare bedroom into a dressing room. We no longer have a garage and don't miss all the stored junk that we used to have. We have also reduced our monthly bills for accommodation and utilities by more than a half of what we spending in the previous house. The savings are now freed up to go into investments for our retirement, further boosting the opportunity for my partner to leave her job in a large organisation and choose instead to reduce her considerable work stress without money being a factor in her decision.

In your own space, what works well and why?

Which elements of your home do you wish were different or more peaceful?

You will be sensitive to the energy of the different rooms in your home and how you feel in each room. In a separate chapter I have written of hoarding and the unease that comes from this and about the awkwardness we feel when our home is a mess. This leads to us reducing our social use of the home and prevents us from having people round.

Taking things one room at a time, where would you choose to start on tidying up your clutter or to begin making more sense of the space you live in?

ELEVEN

Books as clutter

I HAVE ALWAYS loved books and the idea of reducing my books at home has been the hardest issue associated with decluttering and discarding. As soon as I arrived home from the bookstore having seen the book on tidying up and started talking with my partner about the ideas behind living with less, I knew that I would be conflicted about anyone telling me that books were considered clutter. Yet, the sharing of this came not from the author of the book I sat and read in the store but from my better half. She fairly firmly told me that it was not simply unusual to have a house filled with more books than any other object, but actually downright weird! She's a one for subtlety as you can see.

As a young boy books were my friends, just as much as a teddy bear or a box of wooden bricks had been when I was a toddler. The love of books was handed down to me from my Mum who read poetry to me when I was a baby and who introduced me to Rupert the Bear in his annually published collection of stories, to Winnie the Pooh, to Richard Scary and his marvellous drawings of communities populated by animals in the cutest clothes. Then I moved into buying first one or two and then a hundred or more Biggles books by W E Johns. My Dad had managed to save a couple of these from his childhood and I absolutely loved these stories for myself. From here I was moving on to collections of Commando comics, to detective stories by George Simenon and his socially awkward and nonplussed detective Maigret.

As a teenager I would go to the Saturday morning jumble sale in our village hall and come home with an armful of books, feeling as proud as punch with my haul. At university I would buy the recommended reading list for my study year and lose myself in pages opening up the history and exploration of Latin American, revelling in tales of uncovering Mayan temple sites. Home for the summer breaks I would be given vintage copies of stories by H E Bates writing as Flying Officer 'X' and the poetry collections of Walter de la Mare by now elderly neighbours. They were, I now realise, letting go of their own clutter!

Faced with the challenge of decluttering more than thirty five years later I looked at my collection of circa 2,500 books and felt complete dread at the idea of letting go of these. Each book did hold a memory for me. I knew when I had acquired it and often could picture the face of the friend, neighbour or relative who had given it to me. Picking up a volume of childhood stories or a pile of paperbacks left me feeling nostalgic for a past that was long since gone and an early childhood that I had loved so much. Standing in front of a bookcase of 200 books and knowing I needed to whittle it down to perhaps 20 books made me feel physically sick. Several times when I started the process I began to feel light headed and dizzy.

This was because I felt such turmoil, struggling with the distressing reality that I had been accumulating so much weight of books throughout my whole life and that there was no way I could continue with this behaviour. I had hidden the compulsive hoarding as a love of books, avoiding the truth of the problem that surrounded me. No one needs that many books. Quite aside from the volume of titles in my house and storage areas, consider the cost of having acquired them all! It hurt to think that so much had been spent on books, so I console myself with the joy such books have given me over the years.

I had held onto them for nostalgia, for perhaps subconsciously wanting to impress people, for the romantic notion of a writer needing to be surrounded by books. I had let some of the rare books come to me because I considered them a good investment for the future. But all of these reasons are easy to justify. As hoarders or collectors we do this, we make it seem reasonable to have so many of this or that item. They are all just excuses for not being very good at discarding. Perhaps no-one showed us how to discard. I know that was the case for me. Other than a couple of TV shows on the matter I have never had a friend or family member talk me through their own process of decluttering. No one had ever stepped forward to show me how to let go of the accumulated 'stuff of life.'

Elsewhere within this book I delve into the issue of the things that clutter your house representing stagnant energy in one form or another. I know that when I committed to drastically reducing my book stock I felt an instant upsurge in energy, even before I lifted a finger to start moving the books. You will have heard the phrase 'heavy energy' given to rooms or spaces or even to people. Consider the actual physical weight of 100 books, of 200 books. Now think of the emotional energy that is attached to those volumes on your shelves. Does 'heavy' seem like a relevant word for describing the feelings around those books or the space they occupy in your home?

Several hundred books in our house I had not even read, but had bought them on the basis that the cover blurb had intrigued me or the illustrations and maps in some of them had fascinated me. Every single book was taking up some level of my emotional energy and all of them were occupying space that could not be filled by sunshine, or penetrated by music or which took up room that could otherwise allow guests to stay or the house to be easily accessible to visiting friends.

In approaching the challenge of making big inroads to reducing my book stock I found it useful to give some structure to the process of letting go of so much of this particularly emotive theme of the book clutter I had surrounded myself with. I identified six themes which have helped me:

1. Define the Problem
2. Scale Down the Work Ahead
3. Have a Clear Plan for Disposal
4. Notice how You Feel
5. Look after your Health and Well-Being
6. Treat Myself to the things I Cherish

Define the Problem.

Here I needed to walk through the house and look at where books were stored and count the volume. In the garage I had three bookcases, with 180-200 books on each. So 500+ books on shelves. On the garage floor, twelve stacked plastic boxes each with ca 50 books, so another 600 books. In the lounge two tall bookshelves, so another 350 books in the lounge. By my bed, 20 books. In the study and next to my desk, 130 books. In the spare bedroom, 350 books.

In my main office, 500 books across shelves. So about 2,450 in total!

Scale Down the Work Ahead.

My collection was comprised of :

ca 60 poetry volumes

ca 400 books on military history, memoir

ca 50 books on the craft and mindset of writing

ca 50 books on giants, Robin Hood, myths and legends

ca 50 books on self-help

ca 500 novels

ca 100 small business titles

ca 240 travel guides, mountaineering and walking books

ca 1,000 vintage titles such as Ladybird, Observer, Biggles books. Total 2,450. So I knew where everything was and felt better about tackling the overall task. It seemed reasonable to achieve the goal of letting go of more than 2,000 books. But only just!

Have a Clear Plan for Disposal.

I set out to reduce my books to just 10% of what I had around me. This meant that I would go down from ca 2,450 to perhaps 250 books. The goal was a big one and I knew what I had to do in order to manage in a smaller home space and recognise the attraction of spending less on accommodation and putting more into savings and investments. With the 90% that were going to be leaving the house I chose to split these between give-away donations to a local charity shop so they could resell them and use the funds for a worthwhile community project, and to sell just over 1,000 non-fiction books online and see what funds we could achieve via this route. I figured I could list 10 or more books a day online with the intention of seeing these sell via auction. At 70 or more books a week listed online and with perhaps 10 a week actually selling, it would take me close to two years to see all 1,000 books gone and to see a good amount of cash moved into savings.

The titles I would keep would be books that I absolutely adored on my shelves. They had to uplift, inspire, or be directly connected with very special memories of family and friends. To handle each book was the best way for me to approach the disposal and discarding of so much clutter. It was a slow process because I was not going to let go of everything.

By holding each book in my hands I was able to ask myself questions such as:

"Do I cherish this book?",

"Will I read it again?",

"Can I write down my special feelings for this book and let it go?",

"If I really need to look at this again can I find it in a reference library in the future?",

"How did this book enrich my life?"

Being able to fill pages of a journal with the associated feelings for a certain title or to note how I felt about this author, helped me to have confidence in letting go of the book because I knew for sure that I had already received the value of it. It could leave me now.

The easiest for me to let go of were the 500 novels, because I knew that I could find them in my local library or order them in to read if I ever felt the need again. If my local charity shop could resell these for £2 each then they would raise £1,000 from the sales. On top of these another 500 assorted books went to charity, across the range of other themes I had been collecting and potentially raising another £1,000 or more. This is a feel-good result.

Determine what you will keep and enjoy. Give yourself a set time in your diary for each opportunity to declutter and let go. What might you be able to donate this week? How about a similar plan for next week? Will it all be given away or might some of your books be worth selling via an online auction site? Two hundred books at $5 - $10 a piece brings in some useful funds.

Notice How You Feel.

The first time I sat down on a chair next to a bookshelf and with the good intentions of making progress, I found myself thirty minutes later feeling so much love for the books that I could not make any progress. I had placed a cardboard box on the floor by my chair, expecting to fill it with titles I was happy to let go of and it was still empty. My heart was racing and I felt sweaty with just the thought of separating the books into those I was keeping and those which would be discarded. I made some notes about some of the books that I loved on that set of shelves and was aware that I had far less attachment to some books. I could not put anything in the box for the charity shop, but could see that somewhere in my mind I was beginning the process of separating from the attachment to some of the books I had picked up and flipped through.

When you are going to do this, make yourself comfy with a notebook and a pen so you can jot down the feelings, thoughts and memories that pop up. Each time I took a carload of boxed books to the charity shop they welcomed the donation. Yet I received the double benefits of less clutter and feeling good about my donation. At the point you feel nervous or too awkward or uncomfortable letting go of your books, just stop. This is neither a race nor an obligation. The books in your home are just one element of the things that can be reduced to make for a lighter life.

Look after your Health and Well-Being

Have a coffee or a large bottle of water with you as you go through this. You have been so accustomed to having these things with you that the act of potentially letting go will leave you feeling dehydrated and may bring on a tension headache. Doing anything which causes you to feel nervous will make you feel thirsty. Keep yourself hydrated. Play some music you love and treat this as a special appointment with yourself. If it helps to have a friend go through the items with you, invite them over and tell them to bring cake! Start with thirty minutes of removing books from a shelf then stop for a break. Go for a walk around the block. Stretch. Acknowledge the progress first before you do any more clearing of shelves. Consider the progress you make in each short session. Be aware of how you feel.

Treat Yourself to the things you Cherish

When you let go of your clutter make sure to reward yourself for the achievement. My goal when selling the first 200 books online was to acknowledge my decision and the actions by buying an attractive vintage watch that I can wear regularly without taking up much space.

What would you like as a treat for letting go of a mass of heavy energy in your house? It might be a physical gift to yourself like a piece of artwork, some jewellery or a beautiful antique piece. Perhaps it will be a holiday, now that you feel the sense of being able to get away and enjoy yourself.

Whenever you see this item or consider the holiday trip it can serve to remind you of the journey you have been on as you move from hoarding to better enjoying and using the space in your home.

TWELVE

This is all about energy

THE PLACE you call home is a special place because you intentionally chose it. Of course there may be a few exceptions where you were given no option about living there, or because you inherited it. Bummer! Seriously though, you did choose to rent or buy or move to this place which you call your own space, the place you live and where you have stamped your style.

When you stand in the front doorway of this place how do you feel?

On the first day you saw it as an empty space and before you started to bring in your own things, can you recall the emotions you felt as you looked around? It's no accident that you live here.

Sure, there may have been an indirect way by which you made the journey to end up in this location and in this apartment or house, but this is where you are. Deal with it and accept it. Now you can truly make the space your own.

The place you call home is connected with all the

other spaces around you and the world you inhabit. It reflects you by the way you store things there and by what you bring into the home. As your habits and collections and accumulation changes, so too does the mood and energy of the home adapt to this. Your space is a being in the sense that it is a happening, adapting, changing place as a result of how you, your possessions and your guests, visitors and family members interact with it.

Even if the items in the building do not change or swap around for months at a time and the general energy of the house is low, quiet and close to static, you are still moving in the space. The contents of the food cupboards are constantly changing, post is delivered, new items from shopping trips come into the home and other things are used, finished with and removed. In this most basic way there is subtle change each and every day, even though at first glance we might not realise this.

Your home is alive and existing as energy. You are not separate from your home because it is a part of you. It is a reflection of how you think and feel, just as much as you develop by the way you personally interact with the space that is offered to you. The rooms of your home are a representation of how you think and feel, a reflection of your own energy.

Everything in life is composed of energy. Of molecules and tiny atoms clustered together as different forms of 'matter'. Wood and plastic are different materials, but each composed of a set of compressed atoms. Oak, pine, larch and sycamore are all wood types, albeit with a different composition. They each have their own form of energy and this is what you pick up on when you touch the different things in your home. Add to the physical makeup of each item, the emotional energy attached to every piece of furniture, glassware, DIY tool, or art work, books, clothing and bikes. There is a glass bottle on my desk this morning as I write. It is a recycled bottle that has taken other forms before reaching the shop where I bought it and the sparkling water that was in it. There is energy within that static glass structure that I have no control over. It has another energy because I know emotionally that I will be adding it to recycling so it can take on another form once crushed, heated and remade into another glass item.

Also on my desk is a tray with some Coins, a Wristwatch and some Keys. Each item is imbued with a different energy.

The Coins have been in the hands of thousands of people before me. Each has a different date of minting or issue and gives an insight into the potential places they have been used or the times they have been a part of. They have been previously used to buy petrol, scratch cards, lottery tickets, a sandwich, a book, to pay a debt, to buy food, for a bus ticket or a parking token. Every transaction brought energy with it.

The Wristwatch was a fabulous gift on the first Christmas with my partner. She gave it to me with love and made a huge effort to buy it for me. Seeing it after I removed the wrapping paper and opened the box was the most enormous pleasure. It carries those thoughts each time I wear it proudly.

The Keys represent the front doors of houses that

we rent out, each house more than a hundred years old. Some of the houses have been easy for us to improve and repair and rent. Others have been difficult and challenging. Each positive experience, or troublesome event is connected to the key for that front door. With each key are my recollections of the many tenants who have lived in them over time and the relationship or friendship we have enjoyed. You can see now, everything in your home has energy in one form or several.

Look at the Energy in Your Home.

If your home is a place of harmony, love, hope and goodness, then it stands to reason that it should first be a place of sanctuary for you. It needs to be a space where you can be relaxed and completely yourself. For this to happen to the best degree possible you need to tailor the space where you live to meet your own character, aspirations and to work with and support your own value system. This is where you spend your most relaxed time, where you are private and alone, as well as where you can relax with friends and with loved ones. A home is where you can be at your most vulnerable and most intimate. Here you can be completely true to your best you.

To fulfil so many functions energy moves, shifts, surrounds and connects all of the spaces within your home. You are sensitive to light, texture, movement, to stillness, to chatter and to music. In a location where you eat, love, bathe, create, worry, aspire and give momentum to ideas and projects, this connecting energy is everything. Distraction, concerns, low energy, sad areas, fluctuating temperatures, and anything which pulls you from living your best life at home will harm those aspirations, slowing down your creative and communicative elements. These sentient or emotional forms of energy will hold you back from the best. Visual distraction, untidy rooms, chaotic kitchens or unclean bedrooms and living rooms all conspire to prevent you living at your best levels of energy.

You cannot have friends round for drinks or a meal if the space for them is not made special, cleaned and tidied. The visual pull of dirty laundry in a guest bathroom, or of dirty and unwashed crockery on a kitchen surface, or of shoes and coats seemingly abandoned on the hall floor - none of this is good energy. Such presentation of your home space is neither uplifting, welcoming nor special. Why do you tidy up for guests? Why do you want to create a clean and tidy environment for visitors? Forgive me for stating the obvious, but you put effort in so that the energy of your home is positive, welcoming and active for your visitors. That is just the publicly visible elements of your home and the energy associated with those situations.

Just as obvious is the energy present in your private areas of the home. Wardrobes, or laundry basket, or the drawers where you keep your underwear and handkerchiefs, ties and scarves or mufflers. When you open a drawer and it is a disorganised mess, you feel heavy and fed up, knowing that you now have to hunt around to find two separate socks and make a pair. Instead, if you open that same drawer and every separate sock has been paired correctly with it's other half, or your hankies are folded neatly and lined up behind one another and easy to see, how do you feel now? That sensation of ease you get when you know where everything is, this too is energy presenting itself to you. There is much less stagnant energy in the organised drawer or wardrobe. You are helping yourself by lifting the energy in your home. When you are not distracted by mess, clutter or chaos, you have higher energy to be you and to do what you want to do. Faster and with greater focus.

Energy is the movement and vibration between molecules and atoms. It is the stimulation between people. It is the way that a particular piece of music fills a room but also the response it triggers in your brain and emotions as you pick up on the melody or tune in to receive the specific lyrics. You might choose the music when you have a meal with a friend. You would certainly be conscious of the music in your chosen playlist when you have friends around to celebrate a birthday or a special event. You are selecting the energy for the occasion.

In the same way you are bringing energy into your house with the possessions you bring in, with the art you place on the wall, with the fabrics that adorn your furniture. You think you feel good about a box of letters on a shelf in your study that were written to you by a grandparent or a best friend. You occasionally take out an school report that was written about you by a favourite teacher when you were a happy seven year old child and saw the whole world ahead of you.

When you pull up a blanket on a chilly autumnal day and take comfort from knowing it has been made of pieces of fabrics that were once a childhood eiderdown, a grandmother's scarf and a service uniform belonging to a parent, this is good energy. When you look at old photos of a relative you never really liked, but which you feel awkward throwing out - whether for guilt or misguided loyalty - this is low energy that you don't need to hang on to. The colours, the textures and the emotions you attach to the things within every room of your home, all of this, either contributes to or takes away from the energy of your home.

Check your Digital Energy.

If we ever doubted our connection to the world around us, or thought we were separate from the world and living in a bubble, then the great technology advances we have at out fingertips serve to prove the truth of this connectivity. Digital energy is a vast aspect of the energy in our homes. The movement of data, of the pulsing of electrons in and through our home space. We are constantly connected to the external world through our laptops and cell phones. That fast moving, invisible activity consists of data all around us. The advantages are massive and such technology can help us live more positive lives, provide us with home delivery of millions of items - not so good when you are looking to let go of clutter!

You can make contact with friends who lives hundreds of miles away or across the globe. This same data flow provides digital access to jobs where we can find what will suit us, allow us to find a partner through dating apps, give us the edge for investment tips and know-how, or simply allow us to plan a holiday or a trip without the need to go into a travel shop for such information. All of these and a hundred other advantageous uses of technology and connectedness are good for us. But we have to guard against overload on ourselves. You must take care of the potential drain on your personal energy that such digital activities can have.

Why do you feel tired after an hour online just browsing and following digital connections through adverts or social networks, articles or video clips that entertain? Partly because of the huge variety of visual images you see in that hour, but also you feel tired because the energy is moving so fast through and around you. You can be too open to the draining impact of this frenzy. Give yourself set times when you are not online, when you are not connected digitally. You can switch off wifi while you sleep. You can choose to leave your handset in another room when you are spending time with loved ones. You can switch off sound based notifications and limit the time you spend engaged with or sucked in to social media. They are forms of high speed energy and you need to choose whether they contribute to or take from your own levels of energy and aliveness.

Take a Close Look at Your Home.

Thinking about your home space in this way I want you to start to look closely at the energy of the whole place.

The easiest way to do this is to make some time and stand at your front doorway.

How does the door itself look?

Is the surface clean and fresh?

Has it been painted in the last couple of years?

Or is the wood work chipped, the paint cracked and peeling?

If there is a number on the door itself or perhaps to one side, does this look tidy or are any of the individual digits chipped and broken, needing to be replaced with new?

Step through the door and into the first space. This might be a hallway with other doors coming off it, perhaps a corridor, or you could be straight into your living room. Maybe your front door could actually be the entry straight into your kitchen. Stand where you are for fully five minutes. I want you to notice your feelings as you stand here and look at each wall of the room, every piece of furniture, poster or picture or postcard hanging on the wall, at the hall stand or coffee table or sofas. Look at each item and think with your heart about that piece.

Do you like it?

Do you love it?

What memories are associated with it?

How do you feel when you think about the mental pictures and associations you have with that?

This exercise is the first of several for I want to ask you to stand at the doorway to each room in your home and repeat it. A couple of rooms each day is enough because the whole process of looking at each space in your house and considering your thoughts and feeling for each space can be exhausting. Be gentle with yourself as you do this.

Get Your Thoughts on Paper.

Things you can do to make the process complete are to ensure you spend five minutes observing and noticing each space. Then taking your Declutter journal, make notes about what you have seen, what stood out for you or caught your attention. You can bullet point your observations for making more detailed notes later, or you can dive right in and write without hindrance.

Your focus is to notice the energy of each room and how this is created by the furniture and objects within each room. What you feel will be influenced by the colour of the walls, the fabrics of the furniture and decor, by the memories you sense are attached to each item, both the personal and known memories you have of each piece of furniture or item of clothing or the other energies that are there, but which you can only guess at or feel for on the edges of your senses. Whatever you notice, write about it.

Comment on the layout of the room, it's shape and dimensions. Consider how you now feel about the way you have placed furniture and objects within the space. Placement of our things in a home has an enormous significance and can contribute towards or take away from and even block the good energies within our space. With each item coming in to or going out of your house there is an interaction with the greater universe and the world beyond your front door. By looking after the energy that moves around your home through your belongings you will be protecting your own personal energy levels. By looking after yourself first, you are going to see enhancements in the energy of the people who visit you at home, and who then remark on how they feel in the space that you have cleaned, decluttered and given more positive vibration to.

Remember, that when you raise your energy people will always notice. If you want to create greater speed in the way changes happen in your life clean out your whole house or apartment. If you want to see more nice things come into your home energy, take the time to identify the possessions that don't work for you, which don't bring you peace or happiness or joy and let them go elsewhere. They might go to the local waste or garbage site for recycling, they may go to the goodwill to create some positive for a charity wanting to raise funds and reach the new owner with ease. If you seek to create change this can happen best when you let go of what is already forming clutter and representing stagnant energy for you.

You know already that you will be doing this for the whole of your home. It will not be possible for you to complete this exercise and remain neutral or unaffected by what you observe and your feelings as you move around the space. Many things which you have never noticed will jump in front of you to be seen. A lot of materials and textures will become more apparent to you. Sure, you have seen the item thousands of times, but now you will see it in context with what it is placed next to or under or above and you will have a reaction to this placement for the first time. It's all quite natural, for we are so busy in our lives that we can pass by something and not see it for what it really is. We can be absorbed by our activities and not be still enough in our home to be with the things we have brought in to the space.

Taking fully five minutes in each room to observe and notice what is there and how it all interconnects, this will be a helpful exercise in noticing clearly what is in your life. Make your notes and record your observations about each area. Notice how what you write captures or describes the feelings you have in each room.

Which area of the home do you feel happiest in?

Where is the emotional heart of the building?

Which part of the house do you gravitate towards when you feel unwell because in this space you feel cosy, safe and nurtured?

If there is a sad part of the home, where is it, and what makes you feel sad when there? Is it the space or is it an item of furniture or perhaps something displayed on a shelf?

When you have guests to visit do they move naturally to stand and chat in and around the kitchen or an open living area? Do they want to sit outside on the deck with you or gather around a sofa and comfy chairs?

Is there furniture in the house where no one ever sits even when the house is busy? Is this because of the place where the chair is located or is it the chair that people are not comfortable in?

Are there pictures on the walls of your home that you don't like, but have never let go of? Can you understand the emotions that are triggered or blocked when you consider these images?

When you are following a painting or drawing or collecting hobby at home, where do you notice yourself sitting?

How does this area of the living space support you in being comfortable and happy while you follow your hobby?

Why do you think you move naturally to this area to be with the activity you love?

Consider the play of light and shadow of the home and look at how this affects your personal moods and energy levels across the day and in different seasons of the year. Are your rooms organised and laid out for you to get maximum benefit from early morning sunshine and afternoon or evening light?

If you moved a couple of rooms around to take full advantage of the natural warmth and energy from daylight and sunshine, which rooms would be swapped about for your own well being?

THIRTEEN

Letting go of upset

WHY IS it so difficult for us to move through the sadness and heartbreak of a failed relationship and start again? Why do we struggle so much with the ability to feel good about ourself after the thing we were once so excited by has died?

It is tough to move on from something that didn't go the way we expected it to. This could be a job move that went badly and we chose to leave the company or business. It might be a friendship that we thought was going in a certain direction but which was then ended when we were not expecting it to. The biggest heart break can come from when a loving relationship ends and we were unprepared for it. Even when we knew that perhaps, somewhere in our heart, it was not the right thing for us or was a relationship that in various ways may not have been equal and mutually supporting, we still look back on it and wish that it had not ended. Or that it had ended with us being in control. Possibly it finished with a clear bang and not a weak whimper. In any of these scenarios we are still facing the issue of letting go and struggling to know how to do it better.

In our mind we are drawn in to the whole process of *"What if …"* or *"Perhaps I could have …"* Have you ever thought *"Maybe if I had …?"* All you are doing in these cases is replaying the drama and stoking the pain to greater levels than you need to. Remember now, that this is a book about letting go of those things and also the experiences that get in the way of you being your best self.

Do you want to Be Right or do you want to Be Happy?

Can you let go of the sense that you were hard done by when the company let you go, or that you were taken advantage of by your partner in the relationship. Of course, you would have liked to have taken more responsibility at the time in order that the failure of the relationship or the ending of the work had not happened to you. Then surely you would feel better about yourself right now. But that's not how it all happened.

It wasn't your fault! You have been made to look wrong! In your head you want to try and re-edit the history that has already taken place. You put effort and energy into rewriting the script of what actually happened or of the times when you had the opportunity to speak up for yourself but did not. You want to be the person who was right about how things happened or about the decision that was reached, instead of feeling that you were pushed out or dumped or ignored. In all cases you feel the hurt of the outcome that you didn't expect or want to happen.

You can think of the person who did you the harm. You can forgive them for their mistakes against you. How about seeing the whole history re-written such that you are now the innocent one who was not responsible for what took place or for your actions at the time. It can all be airbrushed out of existence or the story retold. This is at least one of the survival methods that are running around in your head. If this is your only plan for recovering from the upset and the sadness, then maybe you need to be open to finding a different approach!

It's a frequently used analogy, but while you are moping around, staying home, criticising things that happened, or feeling sad and angry about what you consider took place, the other person could be out there dancing. Not literally dancing, but living their life and dealing with what is. They could be getting on, moving forward and already have let go. We are different because we are not the same. This is why, for example, four people could live under the same roof at home and have completely different perspectives on what their home life was like as children when they look back on it as adults. I know this is true because I often have the same conversation with my siblings when we meet up and consider our own perspectives on growing up! Try this as an easy experiment. Connect with a couple of your former school friends and get their take on what it was like to be in the same class room as you for several years. Their perspective on the same school and the same room will be completely different to yours.

It is difficult for us to let go because you have to face elements of your own behaviour and your own past actions. If you had made the right decisions earlier then you wouldn't have ended up here in this painful place, right? Wrong! Stop there right now. All these things have already taken place. What happened has happened. You have no scope to have the past be different to the way it took place.

What are your options from here? You could let it all go and admit defeat. You were wrong and you let all these things happen. Someone else was right and you got it wrong. How does that responsibility feel? Fortunately, there is another way for you to approach all of this. You could simply accept what is, let things be the way they are. It can be this simple.

It is what it is.

Your interpretation of an event is simply that, your interpretation. You give meaning to everything. By default you can change that meaning or adapt how you see something by making the decision to do this. You have freewill and choice in the matter.

An example of my own.

I once loved a girl so much that I made up my mind to go and see her and tell her this. I hadn't seen her for three months. I didn't telephone her to say how I was feeling. I didn't write to her and give her any advance warning. Nor had I really ever said anything other than I enjoyed being around her. So one summer I walked 1,000 miles from one side of the country to the other and turned up at her house to surprise her. I walked across vast plains, trekked over steep mountain ranges, swam several rivers, and cut my way through a jungle with my machete. I had considered what I might say when I saw her, I had replayed the scene in my mind a thousand times.

When I got to her place she was delighted to see me, somewhat surprised at my journey, and happy to introduce me to the friends she was staying with and to her boyfriend. The result? I made up a story in my mind that we were not right for each other, that I had enjoyed a great adventure along the way to reaching her house, and that I had other aspects of my journey to give my attention to so I could head off the next day and get on with things. If I hadn't done this I would have become an emotional wreck. Not because of her non-interest, but by my foolishness and naivety in how I had approached all of this from day one. If I hadn't started to see things as they were I would have caused myself enormous hurt. So I very quickly adapted to accept my romantic nature, focussed on the love of adventure and took great pleasure from the accomplishment of the journey through a wild country. Did she ever find out that I had been obsessing about her? Yes, of course she did and a few years later we laughed about it gently as friends and accepted it as part of our joint story, but one she had been completely unaware of.

Here's the thing about accepting what is. You think you were wronged because in your mind, you have told yourself that this really is what happened. Your mind conspires to create a story or to edit a drama in which you were wronged or were made to be the victim in such a situation. It's your mind that does this so of course you must be right, therefore it must be true. I am taking some liberty and license with this in order to make the point. Please don't take this literally. I simply want to help you understand the concept that you can have a story about something in your mind, and if you want to, you can rewrite that story and take different meaning from it. The event sill happened, but you can reframe the meaning you take from it all.

Accepting the idea that an experience is simply what it is, looking at it without judgement, is a powerful way for you to move forward from a place of hurt or upset and to recover the strength and magnificence of who you are. This approach doesn't mean you are giving something up or demeaning yourself at all in the process. But it does allow you to be free of those elements of self-judgement that can taint a scene from your past and add to it all type of negative meaning and, too often, self-criticism. None of this is good for you.

Being Aware is Being Mindful.

Mindfulness is a way of approaching events, people and actions through the lens of non-judgement. In a book about decluttering, about letting go of the things which do not serve you, and the commitments and relationships that do not support you or make you strong or add value to your life, then adopting an approach of mindfulness will potentially be of great help.

Each time you look at a conversation with someone that did not go the way you expected or at a relationship where you feel slighted, insulted or hurt, consider this. Might it be that the other person made those comments or took those actions without the same interpretation that you gave to those same words or actions? If you can see the sense in this or the possibility that this might indeed have been their completely different interpretation of the scene that played out, can you then see that there actually is no right or wrong? Can you see that your judgement and your perspective is just your judgement and perspective, nothing else?

By making a different story about what happened and how you or they reacted to what was said, can you find it easier to process the way you feel about the meaning you took from that event? Might it help you to explore this idea by applying it to some recent hurt or times of unhappiness?

Finding Your Way Forward.

In psychology and self-help books there is a very helpful phrase that comes from the super little book 'Love is Letting Go of Fear', written by Jerold Jampolski. I read this book years ago and always remember his assertion that *'there are only two emotions - Love and Fear.'* At the time I thought that could not be right. What about happiness, excitement, humour, nostalgia? How about panic, terror, nervousness, awkwardness? But the more I thought about his statement, the easier it was to see that so many lesser emotions are simply symptoms of either Fear or Love and that he was right to say this.

Finding it difficult to let go of negative experiences and emotions is difficult because of all the fear that is contained within those same experiences. Put another way, if we were not so scared of what might come after we let go then we would let go so much faster and move forward. Look at this another way, we have a hard time letting go of our suffering because we feel safer hanging on to what is familiar, rather than stepping out into the unknown. Let this go. Step out and know that you will be safe.

Listen to Your Body.

In all that you have gone through and the unhappiness, anger and sadness you have felt, you have given a place to these feelings within yourself. Here is a simple method for loosening those attachments between your mind and body and moving to some resolution that supports the letting go.

Go to a quiet place where you can have half an hour to yourself and will not be disturbed as you go through this practice. You can lie on the floor so long as you are comfortable, or you can sit in a chair that supports you well. Have a notebook and pen nearby because once the physical exercise is done, you will likely find it helpful to make note of your thoughts and observations afterwards.

Start by closing your eyes and taking a cycle of ten steady breaths in and out, just to get yourself to a place where you can work through the process I am going to describe. Once you are feeling calm, think now about the thing you would like to release and to let go of. Think about it, about how it makes you feel, and notice the emotions that come up as you focus upon this.

Take the strongest feeling you can identify and think about where you can find it in your body. All feelings will find a place in our body and create sensations that we are aware of. Perhaps you will feel heat, cold, stinging pain, dull pain, a throbbing sensation, tingling, or even cramp. From your objective self look at the sensation you are aware of. Notice how it is present, what it might look like, how you could describe it.

Now that you are clear on the symptom and where it is showing up in your body, ask yourself if there is a message attached to it. It could be a cloud, or a physical feeling or sensation. Perhaps it is a taste or a smell. Observe what is taking place without judging what is happening. Just let it be. It is what it is, nothing more. Be connected to the sensations that present to you and let them be whatever they are.

Allow the process to continue until you feel that it is done or that you have received the message. Now it is time to repeat that cycle of breathing you did at the start, to relax and find a place of calm and peace. Move through this breathing and then allow yourself to sit up from the floor or to move gently up from your chair. Give yourself a good stretch of your body.

What did you Notice and Feel?

Pick up that notebook or journal and begin to write down what just happened. Write too about your feelings and thoughts of any message or point of release that came up for you in the process you have just taken yourself through. Pen or pencil will be best because you are committing straight to paper through your hand and body. Whatever comes out, just let it do so. Don't pause to edit or to take time out for analysis and judgement. Remember that it is what it is. There is no right or wrong, no crazy, silly or foolish. You are simply being lead to write what comes up and to faithfully record it in the moment. Get close to the whole thing. Keep your pen busy for as long as there is 'stuff' coming up to the surface for you. Let yourself be taken along on tangents as will likely happen. Don't pause to assess whether you should be writing this or that. If it is deep put it on paper. If it is light and funny put it on paper. If it comes up in the thought process or the free-writing that you let happen, then it's worth writing down on paper. Stay with what presents itself through your pen to paper and keep writing for as along as you can or until the connection to the feelings has gone.

I believe that you will have gained value from this process and that the act of writing down the thoughts that surface will give you more steps to moving through your 'stuckness' around the letting go of that situation, scene or interaction with a person. Don't stop there with that first practical process. Do it again next week and the week after. Any time you feel stuck or overwhelmed by the whole letting go process give yourself this private time to breathe, to notice the sensations in your body as they present themselves, and journal about the thoughts, ideas and emotions that come from the physical breathing exercise.

The use of pen and paper in journalling about what comes allows you to go below the conscious thoughts we control ourselves with and take you into a deeper place where you have the opportunity to look at the stronger emotions and reasons which are holding you back into the place where you have been stuck until now. Oftentimes we struggle to change our behaviour and so we keep making the same mistakes because it is easier to do this than face the need for change in the way we approach things. Letting yourself be in touch with the feelings, sometimes painful, of what you did and how you might have done it differently to better care for yourself, all of this takes effort and commitment. Work through this and you will be better able to deal with making decisions that support you in being your best self as you move forward.

What has happened is just that, the past. You cannot change your past. You cannot remove what took place. However, you have the freedom and ability, as well as the means now, to look at the past with a new perspective and with a script that you can totally rewrite to take away guilt and any ill feeling over your actions or struggle. Remember this. It is what it is. Nothing more than this.

You can rewrite your story so that it serves you, rather than pulls you down. Remember this simple phrase, that *"If it's to be, it's up to me."*

When you note down your thoughts from the process, you will likely come up with new ideas for how you live moving forward, fresh approaches to how you enter into new activities and relationships.

How might I see myself differently as a person?

How can I use this experience to identify a new way forward in my life?

What steps can I take to reduce the emotional pain of a similar future experience?

Can I learn from this to let go of upset earlier?

How might I retell myself the story about what I went through?

You are all about what works for you, what makes you happy, and whatever brings you peace. Simply do those things and preserve those items which bring or create or support well being. Let go of the rest.

FOURTEEN

Letting go of toxic people

GIVEN that so much of what we have looked at together this far has been about the energy in your home from objects, possessions and collection, this next section shouldn't be a surprise. It is not about things but about people and how they can have an impact upon us for good or bad, and specifically about letting go of the negative. Toxic people are thankfully a minority but the strength of their effect upon is can be devastating.

In truth it is common for us to go through the letting go process of discarding items from our lives and to find ourselves thinking about some of the relationships that are similarly heavy, unpleasant or even painful. These need to be dealt with for the same reasons that old, damaged or ugly possessions need to be released from our lives, because they cause unhappiness, foster discontent or actually contribute to us being unhappy or unfulfilled.

A good and healthy friendship is one that uplifts, supports and generally adds to the way we live or look at life. In contrast to this a toxic person will bring poison into the relationship, cause us fear, worry or concern. Feuds, fights and arguments are not the characteristics of friendship, but of a strained and difficult relationship that you don't need to be part of. There is no need for you to put up with such a person or to have them in your life. There can be moments in any friendship where there will be times of absence or events that prevent us from being together, but even at this distance the general energy is of help, care and nurturing. Be clear with yourself about any 'friendship' that is less than this to you. You only have so much time and energy in your own life so take the time to focus on - and to be emotionally present in - the relationships which are good for you.

Ask yourself:

What does a good friendship look like?

What value does this person bring into my life?

How do they contribute to our relationship?

How do I feel when I am around them?

Letting go of a friendship that is not supporting you in being your best self is something you need to do in order to live an optimal life, to reduce the distraction of your focus from what matters, but also to stop the drain of your energies. Saying it is one thing though, and actually doing it - making the separation - is another thing completely! We know this, so let's look at some potential ways you can make the break and regain your own energy.

See your Good Relationships as the Benchmark.

Consider why these work, what is good about them, and why there is a natural lightness and ease to the way they are. Seeing the positive ones this way, with an intentional focus, allows you to compare them with the more difficult, awkward and difficult relationships. Look at the amount of your free time you are spending in these good and positive relationships, versus the time you allow to be lost in the ones which bring you no benefit or which actually cause you to feel pain or hurt.

When the Relationship is Not Good for You.

Recognising the truth of this. Face up to the fact that it could be truly toxic. Make a short list on paper or in your mind about why it doesn't work and use this to remind yourself of the actions you are taking. Your friendship might have come to a natural end or you may need to take some practical steps to bring it to a conscious close.

Don't wait for "Sorry".

When a friend has caused you to feel upset, distressed or to feel ignored, don't be the person waiting for an apology. It may never come. Oftentimes the toxic person won't even be aware of the damage they have done to you with their selfish behaviour or sharp words. It seems to be the natural way of things that such people can have low levels of self-awareness. You will just waste time waiting for the expected apology. Move forward. Accept that you need to let it go.

Choose to be around the Good Friends.

These are the people who think about you and consider you for who you are in their lives. Surround yourself with the people who make you feel good. Notice how being with them changes or influences your spirit and boosts your mood. Make an appointment in your diary this week to visit with a friend. Protect and look after this time for the good it brings to each of you.

Ask for Help.

In letting go of the bad ask for help from those friends who can appreciate and understand what you have been going through. You have to let them know what you have been struggling with in that other friendship. The chances are quite high that they have been aware of the situation and waiting on the sidelines to be given permission to step in and help you make changes. Others will not wait to make their concerns heard, and will be stepping forward to be there for you.

Feel the Sadness.

Endings can be difficult and they can be sad. Allow yourself to mourn for the low quality relationship that is ending, if this is what you want to do. Close it down, and let it leave your life. Acknowledge that it did once work well and gave you something you might have needed or wanted at a different time when you were not the person you have since become.

Spend less time in that friendship.

Decline an invite. Leave a gathering earlier than you would have in the past. Simply say '*No*' to an invite. Just because your cell phone rings, do you have to answer it? Let their call go to voicemail. Perhaps reply the next day or not at all, rather than reply within the same hour. Don't respond to a text message or a voicemail at all. Let it go. Be less available than you were before. You can be unavailable for a few invites to meet up. Broaden the time gap of responding to their contact, until one day you have broken the pattern of replying at all.

You could Write to Them.

Don't panic! You don't have to send the letter, but putting your thoughts down on paper can allow them to become more clear than holding them in your head. The simple process of writing a letter can be positive, a cathartic process. See how you feel about the message by reading your words aloud. Have you let go of much of your frustration, anger and discomfort around them, just through the physical action of writing the letter? Do you still want to send it? Perhaps not. So burn or shred it.

Journal and reflect on the separation.

A relationship is about what is shared between the two people. Can you select on what you received and gave in this friendship? Was there imbalance, humour, kindness, fun? The lessons you take from this can be used to help you move forward. Journal as you go through your recollection of the time with this person. Then resolve to let go and move on.

Final Thoughts on This.

The journals that record your good memories, happy experiences or adventures, these are for keeping hold of. This way you can slip into them sometimes. On a cold winter morning you can pull down a journal and read about a sunny day in Mexico or Spain, California or a Greek island. You find yourself transported back there in your mind. You can recall the laughter in the coffee shop, the happy conversation on the beach, the mental stimulation of the time walking round the museum.

With toxic recollection you need to approach things very differently. Once you have used journalling or note making, jotting down your thoughts about that difficult or unpleasant time, get the notes out of your home. Burn old letters that are hateful or cruel. Set fire to a journal of sadness. Let it go.

You are all about what works for you, what makes you happy, and whatever brings you peace. Going forward from here you do only those things and preserve those items which bring or create support and wellbeing.

FIFTEEN

Considering minimalism

IN EXPLORING our own situation of a house filled with 'stuff' and all the emotional issues I felt around these possessions, you know how I started to look at the themes of letting go, of discarding and living with less. You have read about the 'light switch' moment when I was about to buy yet another book and realised the stupidity of doing so, of how that moment started the conversation in my mind about doing the same or better with less possessions and better energy. Let me tell you now about another trigger for me.

I searched online for people choosing to live fulfilling lives with less than they might have had before or for blog articles about frugal living and minimalism. Through such a search I found the documentary called "Minimalism" and sat one evening to watch it. Produced by Matt D'Avella it explores the conversations and ideas discussed by friends Joshua Fields Millburn and Ryan Nicodemus. In looking at this I felt as though I were discovering for myself a previously hinted at, but largely unknown, life space occupied by people who have turned their back on consumerism and instead questioned what they need to live well and to live happily. If Consumerism is the mass wave of being swept along in buying the latest iPhone, or fighting - sometimes literally - for the best deal at a store opening on Black Friday, then the opposite of this is making what you have last longer and being in a place where the same amount of money now buys you more of what you will appreciate and preserve.

I was struck by the stories of different people within the programme and how they had come to a decision based on the stress and fear they were experiencing in what they had previously deemed a normal life along with those of their friends. For example, a broker who had looked up the highest earning categories when he finished school so that he good major in Finance and Accounting at Uni to become a well paid young professional. He had worked for many years and given himself to his company, when one December evening he was told by his boss that he was going to be offered a partnership in the firm after Christmas. The man received this news and then went back into his office and started crying. His moment of clarity came from realising that if he accepted this higher role he would then be caught up in a place of never after being able to walk away from the trappings of the enhanced salary and options, of the politics and status of the role and all that would come with it. He did not like his boss and did not want to see his own behaviour and values change to those that would be an expectation of the newly offered role. That same day he packed up his things from the office and left the building, committed to creating his own freedom by living a life that would be more meaningful to himself.

In another example a lady was diagnosed with MS and faced the shock of this. Her energy levels were down and her ability was hampered by not being able to predict how she would feel from one day to the next. She identified that a lot of her stress was in her possessions and she considered how she might reduce the volume of 'stuff' in their home. For herself she looked at her wardrobe and realised how many clothes and outfits she had which she never wore or wore only very occasionally. She pulled out her favourite clothes and started to give away or to throw way the items she was not using and was not fond of. She identified 33 items of clothing that she kept and, as a trial with herself she began to mix and match those clothes for the next three months at work. No one at her workplace noticed she had massively reduced her wardrobe and so she continued with the experiment, she and her husband letting go of many of their non-essential items. In the process of letting go of so much that brought no value to them, she found that her MS waned and became completely manageable.

A further interviewee is an architect who designs tiny homes. He lives in an off grid trailer unit that can be towed by a vehicle to an alternative site when he chooses. It has a double bed, kitchen, fold down dining table, wifi, solar panels on the roof, a shower room and toilet, as well as shelves for the books he loves. It has good headroom and eaves storage as well.

A man in his twenties shares how he reduced his belongings to just 51 items that he can pack into a weekend shoulder bag and a laptop bag! With just these items he lives a very flexible life, able to work from different places around the world as he chooses, precisely because he doesn't have the baggage that we surround ourselves with in everyday life.

An element of the programme looked at the cost we incur in taking on a large property. One architect made the observation that in a large family home there may well be three dining tables, *"But who can eat a meal at three tables?"* he said. In a monitoring of home usage by thermal cameras the movements of a family around their home were tracked and analysed. The kitchen, lounge and bedrooms were the most used spaces. No one was making much use of a separate dining room, a spare bedroom was never used and the lounge received less use by the whole family than a table in the kitchen area of the house. All of this was done to show that a household does not need the space that we have come to expect in the homes we buy and rent these days compared to the houses that were built and sold forty or more years ago.

We are demanding more space and more facilities in buildings that we make proportionately less use of than our parents and grandparents. Garages are used primarily for storage of clutter rather than for the storage of a vehicle. Rarely are they spaces where we keep our workshop and tool collection. Instead we use such skills less and pay other people to do the repair work for us. The lack of knowledge over how to maintain a house comes at a financial cost. There has been a vast growth in self-store facilities where people pay to have someone else to store their sealed boxes. Often there is a correlation between people deciding to stop paying for long-term storage and their realisation upon collecting the boxes of items, that the things they have stored were not worth the money spent for that same storage hire.

I know this personally and went through much the same thing when, for a two year period following my divorce, I placed a lot of things in the local storage depot. The storage cost was nearly six hundred pounds and I threw away 90% of what I found in that container when I finally managed to pay for it and collect what I had packed in a rush. The whole exercise had been a knee-jerk reaction to moving from a large house to a small space and I had not thought it through. It would have been more cost effective to give away what was predominantly clutter, instead of paying a company to place it in a locker unit for me!

Finance and Construction Working Together.

The mortgage industry and the real estate industry work closely to continue their lending and construction. Rather than buy the home space we need and which is enough for us, the mortgage process encourages a focus on *"How much can I borrow, and what can I get for the deposit monies I have raised?"* The construction company or home developer wants to sell you the largest feasible unit, which serves to lift the profit per property that they offer to the market. This is a far cry from the approach that says *"What space will suit us to live comfortably and without financial pressure?"* The second way of looking at buying a home still allows us to pay down the loan as fast as possible in order to be without debt in those later years when our earning ability is reduced.

In a predominantly subconscious manner we have allowed ourselves to sleepwalk into a place where we spend money on things we don't make much use of. We buy things to replace items that are perfectly functional and still have more years of use in them. We have adapted to values imposed upon the larger society by the advertising messages we are exposed to in books, films, magazines and online and TV advertising. We are captivated by the lure of prestige and status. We find ourselves with debt in the form of loans and or credit card borrowing where we have succumbed to temptation and the glib patter of a salesperson to buy a newer car, or to replace our wardrobe with a whole new rack of things we will not often wear.

Instead, have a car that is five years old and which works fine in getting you from home to work or home to church or home to a holiday destination. It has brakes, seats, wheels and a roof. The lights work and the engine is in good order because it has a decent annual service. You either have no borrowing on it or have made good progress in repaying a loan that you took out to go with the car purchase. Why on earth do you want to take on another larger debt or a new debt to drive a vehicle that is perhaps cleaner and shinier? My guess is that a sense of status and keeping up with the neighbours is what drives that behaviour. Your neighbours are not going to pay for your new car, so I hope you can see the folly of such a purchase.

A new car is one of the least sensible uses of finance because the moment you drive the car away from the dealership it has fallen drastically in price. Just that first mile as you drive off can knock as much as 10 or 20% from the new book value of the car. If your company provide you with a vehicle as part of your compensation package this is a separate matter, but borrowing money to buy a new vehicle for personal use is financial insanity. Within the #debtfreecommunity that I follow and belong to on Instagram it is always wonderful to see and read the stories of people paying down their finance and reducing their debt burden. In our own marketing business we have seen how a young mum with two children has been all to step back from one full-time and two part-time jobs to instead now work her business from home and spend far more time with her children.

The access to cheaper materials and fabrics from the developing world, and the low cost of labour in such producing marketplaces, has allowed us to see disposable or low wear clothing as more affordable than nutritious food. The cost to the planet of the energy required for the creation and global distribution of this level of production has massive consequences. The Minimalists - Joshua and Ryan - are sharing a message that it is better to lead a life where you can rely on far less money because that money will go so much further when spent on items that are durable, and which of course you love and appreciate. When your cost of living drops, but you maintain or enhance that standard of living, you are in a good place. Decluttering and realising what you no longer need is a part of the process of becoming free and gaining greater happiness and contentment with your life.

What I started here in looking at minimalism has again come back round full circle to an assessment of the financial and emotional cost of all the clutter that we can so easily surround ourselves with. It is easy to finance and buy such things, but the regret behind the painful decision can be long lasting and have a heavy toll on our feelings when we face up to the scale of the problem that we have created for ourselves. The less you have around you the freer you are to make quick decisions about changing your life circumstances. This could include moving to another location or being able to let go of a job that drains you and accept a new role or even create one for yourself where you can be happier on less income as you cut your costs and end up living better.

Consider these scenarios:

If you were to be able to make a career change or move to an area that you would love to live in, and you could do this through adjusting your clutter level, where would you be going?

Having considered such a move, what do you think you can do in order to make this a reality?

What will you need to let go of in the process of getting ready for the change of circumstances?

SIXTEEN

The tiny homes movement

IN LOOKING at how we approach decluttering our homes and lives of too many possessions - especially those which get in the way of us being as free as possible to live the life which gives us greatest satisfaction - I have been looking at how our homes can become places that are not just about switching off and unwinding after work.

In a YouTube video about a young Australian writer, Michael Green, I was fascinated to see how he had worked together with his friends and housemates to create a place for him to write, away from the bustle of the house but also overlooking their shared vegetable garden.

A point he made was that he wanted to look at how we often live in and occupy our homes as a place of relief from work, rather than something which is integrated deeply into our values and hopes and which serves as a reflection of who we are. By taking a badly used storage space which had been used as a dumping ground for broken furniture, old suitcases and abandoned junk and placing dedicated effort into turning it into a calm, ordered, space for creativity, something new had been made from the old space. Utility and function has been reborn from recycled materials and given new purpose. He lived in a shared house and wanted to convert an old room in the yard cum garden to be of use as a writing space for himself. His commentary on the video made a strong impression and I watched it several times and then forgot about it.

Since wanting to look more closely at the theme of downsizing or making better use of the space we have around us, I have reconnected with the video again. He has reclaimed a small space, perhaps 9 feet long by 5 feet deep. At the back and sides it has brick walls that have been covered with a double layer of wood lath strips glued at right angles to each other. These have then been been lifted into place to cover the brick work and create an attractive and atmospheric soft brown wall. The front of the shed space has been constructed of an old wood door with multiple glass panes, and a ledge to about four feet high. The remainder of the structure has two large multi-paned windows which can be opened up to let the air in and pegged on wood stilts, creating a real sense of openness to the writing space. By building this creative space as a part of his shared home environment and yet removed from his immediate living space, he has given himself permission to have it as a personal sanctuary. Here he is free to think, reflect and focus on his writing.

I have been deeply struck by the desire of indie

thinkers to make more of their home space, to create something which mirrors their being driven by what matters to them. Whether it is people in the tiny-homes movement choosing to live with so much less than is conventionally accumulated within a house space, or by the minimalists who seek to only have with them those items which receive regular functional use, the whole approach to living with less has triggered something in me and which I can feel is altering how I look at the things which I keep close around me.

What do You Want from Your Home?

Should our homes be serving as an anaesthetic to the varied stress, boredom or pressure of different job roles which we take on? Or can they become intentional places of positive strength and renewal?

We exchange money for our time and in order to show the purpose of our work we buy things to show that the tradeoff has been worth the time spent. This leads to an amassing of belongings in our home spaces and means we spend more on possessions than we place into savings for our future years, when we will not be earning from work and yet expect to have long years in retirement.

Building some element of work function into your home with a space that allows you to operate a small business, a digital venture, a creative endeavour or a means of generating revenue with less stress than relying only upon an employed income, this can only be a good thing.

Shut Up and Write!

At a writing group I attend regularly, a gang of us gather in a tea bar after work hours. We meet from 6pm onwards and for half an hour we chat, catch up on our writing projects with one another, and swap stories of the happenings in our lives. But at 6.30pm our host interrupts the banter to announce, *"Right, it's time. Let's write."* For the next hour we sit close around the tables, sometimes as many as ten or twelve of us. Whether with a laptop, a journal and pens, or loose sheets of paper, we write. Nothing more than this.

We are united by that common desire to capture words, stories and messages on paper and to have these added to each week that we meet. Sometimes I write 500 words in that hour, once I managed 2,002 words and amazed myself. But the act of physically attending the session, the commitment to being there, has boosted my written output and my connection to the craft I love so much. Significantly, it has meant I write more regularly at home and lead me to create a dedicated writing space and routine for myself at home and away from my work hours. Could you create something similar so that you effectively *"Shut Up and Focus!"* on something of real importance and value to your happiness?

Tiny homes and smaller spaces are a part of this drive toward finding form and function in a home and allowing you to look at living better with less. Using #tinyhomes will take you to YouTube videos, documentaries, blogs and online posts all about how you might combine your existing home with a side venture within the home, or to looking at adapting the life you have now to a transition toward the space - both physical in a home place as well as emotional in a mental or productive work space.

Container homes, treehouse living, boat houses and multi-occupied houses might seem extreme and not represent the place you want to move toward. Yet the ideas and the innovation that can come from looking at such communities and thoughts are indeed both helpful and inspirational.

We have reduced by a half the actual square foot area of our living accommodation with the move to our new home, and yet because we have let go of so much that was clutter, we feel better. We feel emotionally richer though from the process of combining more thoughtful living with better use of the space that we do occupy. Financially we are better off to the tune of more than half of what we previously spent on accommodation, utility bills and local authority taxes.

Consider these suggestions:

Can you make better use of your existing home space?

What activity or enjoyable hobby have you let go of at home and why?

If you were to start a new side business from home, is there a place that could serve as a dedicated or flexible space to support your goal?

What can you explore within your community or online to look at more effective use of your home space?

SEVENTEEN

Maintaining your home as a clutter free zone

THIS FAR YOU have made major progress and sorted through so many aspects of your home space, deciding on what goes and what gets to stay in your life for the longer term. I am guessing that when you have been working through the Sell, Donate, Gift or Bin process you have filled many dozens of bags and been able to benefit several charity shops or organisations who are busy with their good works. You may have realised hundreds, possibly thousands of dollars from online sales of good quality clutter that was in need of a new home and to which you had to say a simple 'goodbye'. You have cleared much of the junk and the rubbish from the daily living and sleeping spaces of your home and made a change in the energy of your space. Nice work!

Where do you go from here?

What steps can you take to continue with the good work that has already been done?

How can you manage the space in a way that ends the natural accumulation of clutter?

Keep this Simple!

Easy and uncomplicated actions will protect the good you have already achieved and with less effort than the work you have gone through to get to this new place.

Today, when you look about your home how do you feel about the way the spaces work for you? You need to continue to listen to your heart and to your intuition about the space and what comes in to it and what needs to be moved out every now and then.

Have some key practices to allow you to continue maintaining the space as you want it, one that will support and nurture you.

Acknowledge that things Have Their Place in Your Space.

Plates don't belong in the living room or bedroom. They live in the kitchen. Paperwork belongs in a file cabinet or household paperwork box in a specific area of the home, near to where you sit down to deal with bills, taxes and invoices or expenses.

Post goes in one place in the house, maybe just off the hallway or on a table in that same location once it has come into the house. When post has been opened the envelopes go into a recycling box, not tomorrow or the day after, but as soon as the post has been opened.

Clothes belong in the wardrobes and drawers that

are designed to hold them. Once clothes have been washed and dried they go back into the storage drawers. If you live in a two level house, then things that are to go upstairs but which have found their way downstairs, get placed into a basket or bin by the stairs for moving by whoever goes upstairs next. This is a simple way of ensuring that things get back to their place in the house. Keep the Waste Bin to hand and use this for a regular scan of your surface areas at home. This can be the easiest way to ensure that things don't get misplaced, that clutter finds it difficult to accumulate because you are looking out for it.

Think this is only Your Job?

You can enrol family members into the whole 'keeping tidy' process, but in truth you started this mission and until you have got your head around it first, there is little point trying to press-gang others into the declutter activities until they are emotionally engaged and motivated by living a clutter free lifestyle. You have enough going on in the act of sharing a home, without having to convince your family. Make it easy for yourself and stick with your solo commitment to decluttering until they jump onboard or get excited about it for themselves. Have you ever heard the great phrase *"A person convinced against their will, is of the same opinion still."* I love this wisdom. Get on with owning the declutter process until they join you. They will join you!

Use your Diary and Calendar to keep Letting Go.

Here I want you to track and monitor your own time commitment to the process of watching what is accumulating and to making time to allow things to move-on to their new home, which is away from yours! Having made so much progress by applying the simple steps and actions you have been using from the ideas shared here you can set aside regular planned time to continue the forward progress. Start by allocating a weekly time slot where you can walk around your home and identify things which are not needed. This will not be about simply moving the toys which have ended up in the corridor back to the children's bedroom, or taking plates from the lounge back into the kitchen. These are normal every day activities as part of everyone enjoying the home.

No, this new tracking activity is much more about watching what might be coming into the house as new and which is not as good as you thought it was when you bought it last month. Now you are catching it before it gets dumped in a cupboard and ignored or forgotten for years. This time you are spotting the problem early on, and ensuring the no longer needed item is gone for good to a place where it may be more appreciated or more relevant.

Notice your Shopping Habits.

Another area where you will have massive impact on reducing the clutter is by becoming more aware of what makes the journey into your house. If it doesn't come home then it can't take up space in the first place! On your regular shopping trips into supermarkets, local independent and artisan stores, book shops and departments stores be mindful of what you see that you feel you want for the house. Of course, I am including food shopping here, but more than this I am thinking about the non-food objects such as lamps, cushions, books, fabrics, ornaments, pictures, electrical items and gadgets.

Any one of these can be appealing because they are attractive, or hi-tech, or we feel they are 'must have' items for the living room or bedroom, they are better than what you already have or they represent a prestige element or status symbol for you. Be careful.

Ask yourself :

"How does this new item make a real difference to the quality of my life?"

"Can I have the benefits this item might bring to my home, but for less than the ticket price showing here?"

Could you let go of the some duplicate items you already have and which provide the same function as this new equivalent, but do so before you buy the new item and bring it home? For example, do you perhaps have a couple of hoovers or electrical vacuum cleaners which are old, or actually not working and yet taking up space in your home? Can you let go of these to the goodwill store or the municipal dump before you go out and bring a new device home from the store? So often we see something in a store or online and we buy this as the replacement, but we never get around to removing the original item from our home space.

Support Your Goodwill and Charity Shops.

Prior to reading this book have you regularly donated your good quality unwanted items to a local store where they can resell or repurpose your donation? If not, then can you make this a more regular action for your family or household? This might mean that you now allocate a space in your home to where you store those things which you have already had good value from and which you are considering replacing. Whether this is in a cupboard or on a shelf in the garage doesn't matter. What is important is that each time you have enough things to fill a box then you get this down to the charity shop so they can sell it and recoup the funds for their own good projects. Everyone at home can get involved with this for clean unwanted clothes, kids toys, books, household furniture and kitchen items.

Giving such things a second life can mean an enormous emotional benefit to the person who buys it from the store to make their own living pace better for them. Recycling things this way allows each item to have a second life and is better for you, your neighbourhood and for the planet we all live on.

Congratulate Yourself for the Progress.

Stay with the process of monitoring and watching the level of possessions in your home space. Be mindful of how things arrive in your home and of the items which need to be given away or simply thrown because they no longer have a reuse value.

Consider the declutter journey you have made to get to this point. Look in your journal to see quite how far you have come since starting on this.

Congratulations on the many thing that have gone for good, for the space you have opened up in your home and, of course, for the new energy that has become a part of the way you are able to live now.

Keep doing what you have done and you will continue to reap the rewards of decluttering your home and your life. Well done!

About the author

COLLECTOR OF BOOKS, fan of new reading and ever fascinated with the power of the written world to bring new ideas and thinking.

As an author I love time spent at my desk in my dedicated writing shed at the bottom of the garden or at a table in a neighbourhood coffee shop. I love to be with pens and paper working through ideas for a manuscript or a presentation.

Best of all is getting a concept out of my head and into a conversation with a reader, discussing our different ways of approaching something which unites all of us. This could be around Financial Thinking and Personal Budgeting, dealing with the Clutter we accumulate in our living spaces or wanting solutions and new ways of thinking about Debt so that we can enjoy more control of our money on the way to financial peace of mind.

It is so great to do what I enjoy with the writing,

getting good feedback for the books that people enjoy and which can be seen to be making a positive difference.

Nick Sturgeon

Find Nick at www.nicksturgeonbooks.com

Sign up

SIGN up to Nick's Newsletter for the latest news about his books, subscriber-exclusive offers and freebies. It's absolutely free and you can unsubscribe at any time.

To sign up, go to: nicksturgeonbooks.com/signup

Printed in Great Britain
by Amazon

38241416R00111